D1142204

Collective Bargaining by
Public Employees in Canada:
Five Models

COMPARATIVE STUDIES IN PUBLIC EMPLOYMENT LABOR RELATIONS

Collective Bargaining by Public Employees in Canada: Five Models

H. W. ARTHURS

OSGOODE HALL LAW SCHOOL, YORK UNIVERSITY

ANN ARBOR

INSTITUTE OF LABOR AND INDUSTRIAL RELATIONS

THE UNIVERSITY OF MICHIGAN—WAYNE STATE UNIVERSITY

1971

This monograph is one of a series prepared under the direction of Professors Russell A. Smith and Charles M. Rehmus of The University of Michigan, and is a part of their comparative international study of labor relations in public employment. Financial support of this research project has been derived from a number of sources. Basic grants came from the comparative law research funds of The University of Michigan Law School; the Institute of Labor and Industrial Relations, The University of Michigan—Wayne State University; the comparative economics research funds of The University of Michigan Economics Department; and the research programs of the New York State Public Employment Relations Board and the United States Department of Labor.

Collective Bargaining by Public Employees in Canada: Five Models

Copyright © 1971 by the
Institute of Labor and Industrial Relations
The University of Michigan—Wayne State University

All Rights Reserved

Library of Congress Catalog Card Number: 70-634394

International Standard Book Number:
0-87736-006-5 (paper edition)
0-87736-005-7 (cloth edition)

Printed in the United States of America

HD 8013
C 23
A 7

Preface

THIS study is one of a series of parallel international comparative studies conceived and directed by Professors Russell Smith and Charles Rehmus of The University of Michigan. In addition to my obvious debt to them, and to The University of Michigan through which this study was primarily financed, I also wish to record my gratitude to the Canadian government's Department of Labour Universities Research Committee, which assisted with a generous supporting grant.

Perhaps it was folly to undertake a study of public employee unionism in Canada in the midst of its most turbulent period. Certainly, it has proven impossible to anchor down even basic facts—let alone final conclusions—with the usual weight of footnotes and legislative provisions, of published studies and secondary sources. These simply do not exist. In many places, I must admit, impression has served in lieu of information and anonymous interviewees have been used as the source of missing data. The accuracy of many details thus cannot confidently be guaranteed, although I am prepared to stand behind the overall impressions of the system which I have recorded.

Many persons in official positions with both government and employee organizations were immensely helpful in overcoming the lack of "hard" facts and in guiding me to an understanding of the actualities of the system. I could hardly repay their frankness by disclosing their identity, so that I must ask the reader's indulgence for not doing so.

Three research assistants made invaluable contributions by ferreting out and assembling much information and conducting many interviews: Tom Bastedo, the late Catriona Gibson, and Chris Paliare. To them, my sincere thanks.

The bulk of the research took place during the summer of 1969, and the law is stated, generally, as of November 1, 1969. However, the section relating to the Canadian federal public service has been brought up to date as of March 31, 1970.

H. W. ARTHURS
Professor and Associate Dean
Osgoode Hall Law School
York University, Toronto

943991 ✓

Contents

Preface   v

I.   Background   3

II.   The Private Sector Model: Municipal Employees   15

III.   The Public-Private Model: The Federal Public
Service Staff Relations Act   19

IV.   The Formal Public Sector Model: Collective
Bargaining by Police Forces in Ontario   78

V.   The Informal Public Sector Model: Collective
Bargaining in the Public Service of Ontario   104

VI.   The Professional Model: Collective Bargaining
in the Ontario Schools   131

Collective Bargaining by Public Employees in Canada: Five Models

·I·

Background

PRIVATE SECTOR INDUSTRIAL RELATIONS

THE Canadian system of industrial relations[1] involves two major themes: compulsory conciliation and collective bargaining. The former is the older and the most distinctively Canadian tradition, dating from the late nineteenth century, and has been enshrined in major federal legislation at least since 1907.[2] In essence the premise of this policy was that the community had an interest in preventing, or at least mitigating, the harmful effect of industrial conflict, and ought accordingly to intervene in order to avoid such conflict, if possible. Thus resort to strike or lockout was automatically postponed to permit the intervention of a board of conciliation whose report presumably would be morally coercive, although not legally binding.

However, the more modern policy of encouraging collective bargaining (which was perhaps implicit in the earlier policy) has come to the fore since the mid-1940s. Modern Canadian labor legislation (in each of the provinces and at the federal level) protects the right of employees to organize for the purposes of collective bargaining, enables them to choose a bargaining agent on the basis of majority support, imposes a duty of good faith bargaining upon their employer, and envisages the use of economic power in the event that collective bargaining fails to produce agreement.[3] At least until recently, the survival of the older technique of compulsory conciliation had engrafted upon the collective bargaining system an obligation to delay conflict until the conciliation process was spent, a procedure which was found to be counterproductive in many minor controversies. However, even with the more selective use of conciliation in some Canadian jurisdictions since the mid-1960s, the tradition of avoiding conflict if possible remains characteristic of Canadian industrial relations systems.

In the last quarter century, under the aegis of protective legislation, the unionization of the Canadian work force has grown to approximately 33 percent of all nonagricultural employees. However, in particular industries such as construction, transport, and certain sectors of manufacturing, unionization runs very much higher, while typically in the service and clerical occupations it is of negligible importance.[4]

Much of Canadian industry is owned and controlled by U. S. capital, and approximately 70 percent of all organized workers in Canada in the private sector are members of international unions based in the United States. Thus it might be expected that Canadian unionists would share the traditional diffidence of their American colleagues toward political affiliation and activity. However, Canadian labor does have a long tradition of political involvement (no doubt rooted in the British experience of many of its early leaders) which came to fruition in the 1960s with the creation of the New Democratic Party, to which many union locals are affiliated. However, the New Democratic Party has remained a third party on the national political scene, and accordingly Canadian unions are left to influence national political policies in the traditional North American manner by lobbying, by presenting briefs and submissions on a periodic basis to government, and by attracting the sympathetic attention of friendly members of Parliament.

Only in British Columbia (the most heavily unionized province), Manitoba, and to some extent in the industrial heartland of Ontario has direct labor political activity reached significant levels. Thus it can fairly be inferred that the basic concerns of most Canadian unionists lie in the realm of collective bargaining, and it is by this means that most seek to accomplish their objectives. It is true that on a few occasions, exasperation with the collective bargaining process, or with its legislative or administrative framework, has led to threats of a general strike or to more purely symbolic forms of protest. However, except for the Winnipeg general strike of 1919 and a few political strikes in the 1930s and 1940s, there has been no significant tradition of recourse to direct industrial action by unionists for noncollective bargaining objectives, other than by way of dramatic local gestures, such as parades or demonstrations.

This is not to deny, however, that on occasion collective bargaining strikes have had such significant consequences for the community or the nation that they have resulted in some unusual form of legislative or administrative intervention. It might even be conceded that such intervention was within the contemplation of the strikers from the outset. Yet the objectives were essentially nonpolitical and related to the winning of improved wages and working conditions.

Subject to these preliminary qualifications, the private sector labor relations system in Canada, as in the United States, has as its main preoccupation the promotion of collective bargaining. Legislative provisions and judge-made rules differ of course in many particulars, even as between various Canadian provinces and the federal sphere. Levels of sophistication differ as between industries and different parts of the country. But in the main the Canadian industrial relations system may properly be characterized as North American.

TRENDS IN CANADIAN PUBLIC EMPLOYMENT AND IMPLICATIONS FOR COLLECTIVE BARGAINING

It is rash to attempt to characterize the ethos of public employment in Canada in a word or phrase. The traditions and prestige of public employment have evolved over a century or more and are now in a period of particularly rapid change; they embrace various categories of employees from blue-collar workers and lowly clerks to sophisticated professionals and powerful administrators. The work situation of public employees spans a wide range of urban and rural settings in Canada and abroad, and they involve the discharge of the functions of three levels of government—national, provincial, and municipal.

But conceding the inherent folly of the exercise, it is still possible to venture a few generalities about what it means to be a public servant in Canada. In the first place, the state is generally regarded with neither awe nor hostility; its employees do not, therefore, automatically bask in its prestige nor do they sacrifice their own status by accepting public jobs. Second, political patronage has been largely eliminated from the federal civil service over the past fifty years, but the unsavory practices of an earlier era and the continuation of patronage in some provinces and municipalities do to some degree continue to cast their shadow over government employment even today. Third, partly a reaction to the patronage system, partly a reflection of the difficulty of measuring governmental efficiency by business standards, partly a result of using government as an employer of last resort, rigid systems of classification and promotion developed and combined with a reluctance to discharge employees to virtually confer life tenure upon federal and provincial civil servants. The resulting emphasis on security as a distinctive feature of government jobs has perhaps tended to attract less aggressive and ambitious individuals to such jobs and to inhibit the recruitment and retention of those who put a higher premium on opportunity than security. Such, at least, is a common image of the civil service, however justified it may be on the facts.[5] On the other hand, a recent study of occupational prestige in Canada discloses that relatively high prestige attaches to public employment, particularly in relation to other semiskilled and blue-collar jobs.[6]

The implications of these images of the public servant for the practice of collective bargaining invite speculation. It would seem that if the state were to be regarded with awe and if service on behalf of the state were considered a privilege, there would be some reluctance to challenge the public employer's authority through collective bargaining. However, if the attractiveness of government employment is attributable only to the availability of jobs for those who cannot find them elsewhere or to wages, working conditions, and security of tenure which are superior to those available elsewhere, it would seem plausible that government employment relations would reflect the tensions and traditions of the general labor market. For example, as private sector wage levels and conditions of work become relatively more attractive, public servants might either seek private employment or turn to private sector expedients to recapture their former preferred position.

But perhaps more important than these rather generalized and speculative considerations are certain inferences which may be drawn from an analysis of trends in the size and composition of the public sector work force.[7] Paralleling a dramatic population increase, the rapid rate of urbanization, and the growth of the positive state, the scope and size of government employment in Canada has increased markedly since World War II. Some notion of the scope of the increase is revealed by the following figures:

Year	Federal	Provincial	Municipal	Total
1946	116,657	50,041	56,760	223,458
1956	155,892	108,775	101,942	366,609
1966	228,325	257,115	224,715	710,155

In other words, total government employment in Canada has more than tripled over a period of approximately two decades. What is particularly significant is that the rate of growth at the federal level has barely doubled and now appears to be entering a period of decline, while provincial government employment has multiplied fivefold and municipal employment fourfold.

These gross statistics, moreover, tend to conceal another development: the qualitative change in the composition of the work force in the direction of a much higher percentage of administrative, professional, and technical personnel. The diminishing importance, at least in relative terms, of clerical and operational personnel is even more pronounced than in the private sector. Faced with the need to recruit, retain, and replenish these well-educated and well-qualified cadres, governments are increasingly obliged to improve the "image" of public employment and to provide career opportunities which are competitive with those in the private sector.

What is the significance of these developments for public service collective bargaining in Canada? First, although the provincial civil services have expanded at the most rapid rate, the provinces, of the three levels of government, have moved most slowly in the direction of normal private sector model collective bargaining practices. While municipal labor relations are now to all intents and purposes conducted under labor relations statutes of general application, and while the Public Service Staff Relations Act at the federal level has created a congenial legislative framework for collective bargaining, few provincial governments have followed Saskatchewan's early lead and accepted the private sector model for their own labor relations. Thus the focus of controversy in public service collective bargaining is likely to be located at the provincial level over the next decade. This is not to suggest that the federal legislation will automatically solve all differences between the government and its employees, or that all municipal governments and their employees have utilized the opportunities for collective bargaining afforded by the legislation. But at least at the federal and municipal levels, if only in a few provinces, the basic policy decisions have now been taken and are unlikely to be reversed. Pursuit of this theme will be a major concern of this study.

A second implication for Canadian public service collective bargaining relates to the impact of collective bargaining upon key groups of publicly employed professionals and of their impact upon the collective bargaining process in both the public and private sectors. In this respect the early experience of the federal public service appears to be that many professional groups will in fact seize the opportunity to engage in collective bargaining activities and (if Quebec provides a lesson of general significance) may even become extremely militant. To what extent professionals will come to perceive themselves, and to be perceived, as part of a labor movement which, in the private sector, continues to be virtually devoid of even white-collar employees, let alone professionals, is problematical. More likely the unionization of government professionals is likely to lead to parallel developments in the private sector, with both groups of professionals maintaining an arm's-length relationship with the general body of the labor movement. Nonetheless, as leading employers (and sometimes the only employers) of professional, scientific, and technical employees, governments are bound to influence developments elsewhere.

A third consequence of the increase in the numbers of

public employees, especially at the scientific, professional, and executive levels, is the drive for quality and efficiency. As has been suggested, government employment has suffered, rightly or wrongly, from an image of political patronage, inefficiency, and deadening security. At the senior levels, at least in the federal government, an exclusive circle of "mandarins" was believed to dominate,[8] while in many provincial and municipal governments the dead hand of seniority and status quo-ism thwarted initiative. To be sure, this picture of public employment may not have been entirely justified by the facts, especially after 1945, but it did tend to operate as a self-fulfilling prophecy, by impairing recruitment into the public service. However, under pressure for personnel of high competence to perform the complex tasks of modern government and in the face of ever-increasing tax burdens which make efficiency imperative, governments have moved to change both the actual tempo of public employment and its image. For example, in announcing a 10 percent reduction (largely through attrition) in the federal civil service, Prime Minister Trudeau stated: "We want to have improved management of human resources in order to obtain more from our public service employees and this is natural. They have higher salaries; the taxpayer is paying more for them and they will have to produce more. Greater efficiency will replace greater numbers."[9]

Coupled with a call for wage restraint by organized employees, the implications of this position for collective bargaining are clear: public employees have been put on notice that they must be concerned about the very existence of their jobs, about new work standards which they will be expected to meet, and about the dim prospects for significant pay increases. Their response was predicted by the leader of the major public service union: "The president of the Public Service Alliance of Canada warned last night that the new civil service chop could 'push many civil service bargaining units into a strike position.' Claude Edwards, president of the 120,000 member alliance, said large-scale layoffs could lead to demands for 'iron-clad' security of employment clauses in future contracts."[10]

These developments, which have their counterparts at all levels of government, have combined to produce in the public sector an atmosphere in which not only is collective bargaining seen as inevitable, but in which a high degree of militancy is predictable, even among formerly quiescent groups.

Against this background, it is now possible to explore the development of Canadian public sector industrial relations policies. In brief, the trend has been toward "normalization" of the public sector, toward the evolution of a system of collective bargaining which in all essential respects resembles that in the private sector. In order to trace this evolution, what will be attempted is not a complete review of all experience in the public sector in Canada, but rather an account of recent experience at the federal and provincial levels, with special reference to Ontario, and selective examination of other provincial systems. These rather arbitrary provincial parameters have some practical justification. Ontario is the most populous and heterogeneous of the ten provinces, comprising about one third of Canada's total population. Its labor relations traditions are more in the mainstream of North American development, reflecting, for example, neither the national and social convulsions of Quebec, the radical-reactionary confrontations of the west coast province of British Columbia, nor the influences of the fishing and agricultural economies of the maritime and prairie provinces. On the spectrum of the provinces, Ontario ranks neither as the most conservative nor as the most innovative.

Most importantly, Ontario and federal legislation encompass examples of each of the five main models of public employee collective bargaining systems found in Canada.

These models may be characterized as follows:

1. *The private sector model:* the outright application of private sector collective bargaining legislation to public employees.

2. *The public-private model:* private sector collective bargaining principles, procedures, and institutions are replicated in a distinctive public sector system, with or without modifications as to detail.

3. *The formal public sector model:* a distinctive statute for public employees, which provides for formal negotiation procedures, collective agreements, and arbitration or some analogous device as a final and authoritative procedure for the resolution of disputes.

4. *The informal public sector model:* a distinctive statute, or informal tradition, which permits consultation or negotiation between a government and its employees and establishes some method of dispute resolution, but does not envisage the execution of formal collective agreements or the making of binding arbitral awards.

5. *The professional model:* a professional group of public employees enjoys powers of self-government which are employed both to secure individual professional standards and to advance group economic interests through lobbying, consultation, and negotiation.

In the following chapters, an analysis will be made of each of these models and of its application to particular groups of public employees.

THE POSITION OF GOVERNMENT AS AN EMPLOYER

The range of statutory and informal procedures listed above, often surprising to foreign observers, reflects Canadian constitutional practice and theory.

First, in theory the legislature is supreme, subject only to the division of legislative powers within the federal system as between provincial and national governments. Thus while the executive (in Canadian parlance "the crown") enjoyed legal immunities at common law, these immunities were liable to be—and have increasingly been—overridden by the expedient of a simple statute. In the realm of public employment, the potential importance of this principle was illustrated in Saskatchewan in 1944, when the provincial government brought its employees under the general private sector labor relations act by providing an appropriately inclusive definition of an "employee" in the statute.[11]

The real question, then, is whether or not the legislature

wishes to preserve or abandon government's traditional freedom of unilateral action. As one leading Canadian scholar has observed, the answer to this question is not found in the realm of constitutional theory so much as "in the interplay of individual and group pressures which decisively influences the course of state action and produces the sovereign will."[12]

In Canada this "interplay" has been evident in a wide variety of citizen-state controversies and has produced a progressive broadening of governmental accountability for the actions of the executive. The nexus between government-as-ordinary-citizen for purposes of actions in tort or contract and government-as-ordinary-citizen for purposes of employment relations has been eloquently suggested:

> The people as sovereign may consider itself unsuable, or it may allow itself to be sued. It may permit itself to be bound by "contracts" with private firms, or it may decide not only to ignore the contract but to confiscate the physical and financial resources of the firms. It may hold its civil servants in virtual bondage—recruit them by conscription and maintain them in monastic isolation; or it may grant them the right of association, provide channels for mutual consultation, and even, if it wills, accept as binding the recommendations of a tribunal which owes its existence to the sovereign's caprice. One can pursue the theoretical argument to its logical conclusion, but it becomes a reductio ad absurdum in relation to experience. The fact is that the concept of sovereignty may be defined so narrowly or so broadly that almost any kind of practical adjustment is possible.[13]

The concept of "sovereignty," then, does not present a genuine obstacle to the enactment of almost any legislative scheme for public employment relations to which a government might wish to commit itself. This is not to deny, however, that it does occasionally form part of the rhetoric of debate or the tactics of negotiation. As to the former, "sovereignty" has sometimes been the slogan of those who are anxious to preclude collective bargaining by public employees so that government can continue to determine unilaterally its spending priorities and employment policies.[14] As to the latter, public sector negotiators must no doubt be aware that Parliament always retains the right to amend legislation, and might in a genuine national crisis assert "sovereignty" (in the limited sense) to amend a statute whose constraints seemed unbearable.

A second consideration flows from the political relationship of the legislature to the executive in a parliamentary system of government. By constitutional custom, the executive is controlled by the party which enjoys the support of a majority in the legislature. Coupled with the fact that party discipline is strong, in practice this means that the executive controls the legislative process, although constitutional theory would imply that the executive is subordinate. It would be unthinkable, then, for the legislature to refuse to honor an agreement negotiated by representatives of the government. Of course, as in the presidential system, the appropriation of funds ultimately is the prerogative of the legislators, but they could only refuse to honor the commitment of the executive at the cost of bringing down the government and precipitating an election.

A third constitutional consideration relates to the position of municipalities in Canadian law. "Municipal corporations," as they are properly called, were never regarded as sovereign political entities; rather they were creatures of provincial legislation, enjoying only such power as might be delegated to them by the province and enjoying only those immunities conferred by the province.[15] Thus, as a legal matter, there was no obstacle to the inclusion of municipalities within the ambit of general labor relations statutes: unless they were expressly excluded, they were deemed to be included. As will be seen, some provincial legislatures were initially prepared to license such exclusion, although the present position in almost every province is that municipal labor relations are governed by private sector statutes.

Finally, there must be considered the status of employees of government-owned proprietary industries. From the enactment of the first significant collective bargaining legislation in

Canada in 1907, the federal Industrial Disputes Investigation Act, no distinction was drawn between government-owned proprietary industries and those which were privately owned. In a country where one of the two national railway systems, one of the two major airlines, one of the two national broadcasting networks, and a host of local utilities and services are all publicly owned, the resulting widespread unionization of employees whose ultimate employer was the government helped to open the door to normalization of labor relations policies within the civil service proper.

To mention some concrete examples at the federal level, Canadian National Railway, Air Canada, and the Canadian Broadcasting Corporation were unionized under private sector legislation, as were crown corporations such as Polymer Limited and Atomic Energy of Canada Limited. Provincially, such giant enterprises as Ontario Hydro and Hydro Quebec, Saskatchewan Power Corporation, and the provincially owned Ontario Northland Railway are all unionized. Most municipally owned transit systems and public utility companies in major cities are also unionized.

The main group of industries and agencies excluded from the reach of private sector collective bargaining legislation are those designated as "crown agencies."[16] These agencies include (by specific definition) such operations as a government-owned warehouse, the workmen's compensation board, and a government radio station. Whether provincial universities fall within the same category has been a matter of litigation which has produced a conflict of judicial views.[17]

The ability of government to act as an ordinary employer, then, was relatively unencumbered either by constitutional complications or by inhibitions caused by lack of experience. While there are real problems, these largely stem from the difficult technical tasks of designing and administering fair and workable labor relations policies in the public sector. To the examination of these tasks, the balance of this study is devoted.

·II·

The Private Sector Model: Municipal Employees

A S indicated above, Canadian constitutional law views municipal corporations as the creatures of statute; they possess neither inherent powers nor sovereign immunities. Accordingly, in the absence of a specific exclusionary provision, municipalities will fall within the ambit of a general labor relations statute. In Ontario, for example, such an exclusion existed at one time, but by the mid-1960s municipal labor relations were brought under private sector legislation in almost every Canadian province, including Ontario.[1] However, a variety of special procedures exist which regulate the right to strike of municipal employees engaged in essential industries.[2]

In Ontario some municipal employees have apparently practiced collective bargaining at least since the 1920s.[3] When modern legislation in the style of the American Wagner Act was first introduced in the mid-1940s, municipal employees were among the early groups to claim its protection. Thus the present relationship in such large urban centers as Toronto has developed over a quarter-century or more.

In all respects, as indicated, municipal employees fall under the ordinary private sector statute: they are guaranteed the right to organize and bargain collectively; they are entitled to be represented by a union which may seek certification on the basis of majority support in an appropriate bargaining unit; following good faith bargaining and compliance with the general requirement of exhausting the statutory conciliation procedures, they may lawfully engage in strikes; and they may enter into binding collective agreements which are enforceable through conventional grievance procedures and arbitration.

Obviously, however, the working out of these procedures in the special environment of municipal government has posed certain practical problems. Thus in defining the appropriate bargaining units for civic employees, it has been necessary to establish certain tests for "community of interest" among those included. In the major Toronto area municipalities, for example, there are separate "inside" (white-collar) and "outside" (blue-collar) units.[4]

What is of particular interest is the bargaining process and the process of dispute settlement. Unlike the private business corporation, the municipal employer operates under a variety of constraints: the limited opportunities for increasing revenues to meet increased labor costs; the absence of clear authority vested in a particular spokesman to negotiate and conclude a collective agreement; the political reaction of the public to the costs of settlement or the inconvenience of a strike. Each of these deserves review.

Usually a large Ontario municipality will be governed by an elected council with either an executive committee elected by the aldermen from among their number or a board of control elected on a municipality-wide basis. The mayor, although a member of the board of control or executive committee, has no independent executive power or, indeed, any special political power other than that derived from the force of his personality or of his municipality-wide electoral mandate. Accordingly, all decisions must ultimately be made by the council itself, although a two-thirds majority is required to overturn decisions of the executive committee or board of control. This governmental structure molds the collective bargaining procedure of the municipal employer.

Typically, the employer negotiating team comprises the mayor, some or all of the executive committee members or controllers, and senior management and financial officials of the municipality. In preparation for negotiations (which do not occur on any statutorily determined cycle) the annual municipal budget estimates will be prepared with possible increases in view. These will be concealed from the union by the nonsegregation of wage and other items in the budget finally approved by council, and by the establishment in that budget of unidentified reserves. As negotiations approach, the employer position will be determined more closely, usually by secret deliberations of council.

Negotiations proceed in the normal fashion of the private sector with no overt attempt by the union to mount direct political pressure to bear on the council. To some extent this forbearance is explained by the absence of party politics in Canadian urban governments, and by the fact that negotiations will seldom be close enough to elections to provide a convenient occasion for such pressure. On the other hand, members of council are no doubt aware that civic employees have long memories and that they might be able to tilt the electoral balance in civic elections in which voter turnout is traditionally low—about 35 percent or less. Thus, the use of political leverage cannot be altogether discounted.

Following negotiations, of course, council must ratify any agreement reached by the management team. The reasonable flexibility of municipal budgets facilitates this process of ratification. In Ontario the upper limit of the tax rate which must be struck to pay for any wage increase is not determined by statute or referendum. The only recourse of voters who must bear the heavy tax burden occasioned by overgenerous wage settlements is to vote the council out of office at the next election. Indeed, even the fact that a tax rate has been struck, and the taxes collected, does not unduly inhibit the ability of the municipality to meet the costs of settlement. As indicated, there is some flexibility within the budget estimates so that funds can be shifted from nonwage to wage items; moreover, reserves and contingency funds can be tapped. Perhaps most important, municipalities may, if driven to it, engage to a limited degree in short-term deficit financing to meet current operational costs, although the practice is probably illegal.

This is not to say that Ontario municipal employers have been free-spending or over-generous. Collective bargaining is inevitably difficult, and even those members of council who are politically prolabor usually take a firm stance in negotiations. Over the years the larger centers have developed benchmarks, often by mutual agreement between the parties, which establish the framework of demands and counterproposals. These benchmarks look to rates paid both by other municipal employers and by a sample of private sector firms. Naturally they are not binding on either party, and the level of settlement reflects the relative strength of the two sides, as in the private sector.[5]

There are no inhibitions on the right of Ontario municipal employees to strike, other than the general requirement that the conciliation procedures provided by the Labour Relations Act be exhausted.[6] On several occasions in recent years this right has been exercised, as for example in 1966 and 1968 when the Toronto "outside" workers struck. Although these strikes potentially posed a serious threat to the community, since the employees involved included garbagemen and operators of the sewage and water supply systems, in fact no danger ensued. In 1966 key functions were maintained in the sewage and water plants by supervisors, in 1968 by union-arranged emergency crews. In 1966 cold weather prevented the spoilage of garbage, while in 1968 polyethylene bags were distributed to homeowners, who either retained the garbage for the one week duration of the strike or deposited it in predesignated dumps in city parks.

On only one occasion has the Ontario government actually intervened, by ad hoc legislation to require compulsory arbitration of a threatened strike of municipal hydroelectric employees.[8] In this respect Ontario has acted in a much more restrained fashion than other provinces, which have enacted statutes containing permanent procedures for preventing strikes by municipal (or other) employees engaged in providing essential services.[9]

Perhaps the most impressive fact about Canadian municipal labor relations is that the system operates in a reasonably "normal" fashion. In that sense it hardly presents as interesting a picture as other areas of public employment, which are characterized by more novel statutory arrangements.

·III·

The Public-Private Model: The Federal Public Service[1]

IN March 1967 labor-management relations in the public service of Canada entered a new era with the enactment of the federal Public Service Staff Relations Act.[2] In a country whose social and economic policies have been stamped with an indelible tone of moderation and whose labor policies have hitherto been largely derivative, the new statute must be regarded as profoundly significant. It established for employees of the Canadian federal government a system of collective bargaining which in all essential respects parallels that prevailing in the private sector: exclusive representation rights for unions selected by a majority of employees in a bargaining unit; prohibition of employer unfair practices; an obligation to bargain in good faith; a right to strike which is inhibited only slightly by considerations of national safety or security; and binding collective agreements which are enforceable through arbitration.

THE BACKGROUND OF COLLECTIVE BARGAINING IN THE CANADIAN PUBLIC SERVICE[3]

Employee organization in the Canadian public service began in 1889 with the establishment of the Railway Mail Clerks Association.[4] Postal employees soon formed similar organizations, and within twenty years significant beginnings of a general civil service association had emerged; by 1920 even professional employees had formed an association. However, no significant formal machinery for labor-management consultation at the federal level appeared until 1944. In that year the federal government created the National Joint Council of the Public Service of Canada to advise it on wages and working conditions for its employees. Other bipartite advisory groups were established in the succeeding years. One of the most important was the Pay Research Bureau, whose function is the development of benchmarks for public employment conditions based on carefully selected private equivalences.[5] Institutionally, the federal government's agreement in 1953 to the voluntary, revocable checkoff of dues strengthened the various employee organizations.

Whatever else these years of development represented, by the early 1960s there was not yet a system of collective bargaining in the public service. The federal government continued to act unilaterally in fixing wages for its employees, although it was ostensibly committed to accepting the guidance of the Civil Service Commission. The commission, in turn, engaged in consultation with the employee associations—initially on an informal basis, but after 1961 pursuant to a statutory mandate.[6] Needless to say, neither the strike weapon nor arbitration was considered an appropriate dispute resolution mechanism when the Civil Service Commission and employee representatives failed to agree in the course of such consultations. Moreover, no formal mechanism had emerged which authoritatively determined the right of employee associations to speak on behalf of federal civil servants or which protected their right to join and participate in such associations. However, it was not the lack of a legal mechanism for regulating relations between the Civil Service Commission and the employee associations which proved to be the fatal deficiency in this system. Rather, it was the fact that the Civil Service Commission had the power only to recommend to the federal government that the terms of employment agreed upon in consultation be implemented.

In 1963 the Conservative government then in power rejected a pay increase recommended by the Civil Service Commission after discussions with the employee associations. This action precipitated a crisis in public service employment relations at the federal level. By chance this crisis coincided with a crisis in the political fortunes of the Conservative Party; soon afterward the government fell and a national election ensued. Since it followed the government's rejection of the "negotiated" recommendations of the Civil Service Commission, the election provided a convenient occasion for the discussion of full-blown collective bargaining rights for federal public servants. Each of the three major political parties responded to public inquiries from the civil service unions by supporting a system of collective bargaining in which compulsory arbitration would be used to resolve negotiation impasses. The Liberal Party won the 1963 election and soon after taking office appointed the Preparatory Committee on Collective Bargaining in the Public Service to investigate the technical problems of fulfilling its election pledge.

One particular feature of the new Liberal cabinet must be mentioned here, because it helps to explain not only the forthright discharge of an election promise, but also the nature of the committee appointed. The prime minister, Lester Pearson, was himself a former civil servant, as were a number of his senior cabinet ministers. Given this affinity between the political leaders of the country and their former colleagues in the federal civil service, it is not surprising that they took immediate steps to harmonize government-employee relations. Similarly, it is not surprising that the committee appointed for the purpose of executing this mission was composed almost entirely of senior public servants. The chairman of the Preparatory Committee, Mr. A. D. P. Heeney, was an outstanding and widely respected civil servant who had served the government of Canada for almost thirty years; other members of the committee included the chairman of the Civil Service Commission, the secretary of the Treasury Board, and senior management-level civil servants from a number of other important government departments. In addition, the Preparatory Committee sought and obtained assistance from a number of academic experts, management and labor professionals, and respected labor neutrals. Of course the committee also consulted actively with various employee associations in the public service and with the national labor centers.

The Preparatory Committee saw its task as essentially a technical one: how best might collective bargaining be implemented in the public service? Virtually absent from the committee's report (and presumably also from its deliberations) was any discussion of the fundamental, underlying political issue of whether public servants should be permitted to engage in the process of collective bargaining. This issue was taken to have been settled by the events of the preceding months. Accordingly, the committee recommended in July 1965 a complete system of collective bargaining for all federal government departments and agencies not falling within the scope of the general federal labor relations statute applicable to private employers and certain public service enterprises.[7] The committee proposed binding arbitration as the method of impasse resolution for both grievances and interest disputes.

However well conceived this system of compulsory arbitration might have been, a successful, if extralegal, postal strike rendered it obsolete within a matter of weeks. This strike drastically transformed the attitudes of both employers and employee representatives toward the recommendations of the Preparatory Committee.

In its report, the committee had declined to recommend an explicit legislative prohibition against public employee strikes:

> Looking at the recent history of the Public Service, we concluded that it would be difficult to justify a prohibition on grounds of demonstrated need. We concluded also that, if a strike should ever occur, the Government would not be without means to cope with it. At the present time, most of the employees to whom the proposed system would apply do not have a "right to strike" and would be subject to disciplinary action by the employer if they were to participate in a strike. Nothing in the recommendations of the Committee is intended to change the position.[8]

The postal strike revealed the unintentional irony of this statement. Considerable public sympathy for the strikers forced the government to appoint, as "the means to cope with the strike," a fact-finding commission which largely vindicated the postal workers' position. Although the Preparatory Committee had pointed out that public service strikers would not be exercising a "right to strike"[9] and would theoretically be subject to disciplinary action, the government realized that it could not, as a practical matter, suspend or discharge thousands of employees. Consequently, it confronted the necessity of thinking the unthinkable and legalizing the illegal. At the same time, the success of the postal strike and the growing identification of public employees with the main body of the Canadian labor movement combined to persuade other civil service employee associations to demand the right to strike instead of compulsory arbitration. They were supported by private sector unions, undoubtedly anxious to avoid the precedent of a statute denying the right to strike, who vigorously protested the proposals for compulsory arbitration.[10]

As a result of this pressure, the recommendations of the Preparatory Committee were substantially modified in the course of preparing a bill for consideration by Parliament. When draft legislation was ultimately introduced it contained a novel formula under which a union could elect to resolve collective bargaining impasses by resort either to binding arbitration or to strike.[11] After appropriate preliminary formalities, the draft statute was sent to a joint committee of the Senate and House of Commons for study.

Since a parliamentary majority continued to elude the Liberal government, which held a mere plurality rather than a majority of seats, there was a risk that the deliberations of the joint committee on this controversial measure might be used for political harassment. However, a genuine nonpartisan atmosphere prevailed. The legislators sought and weighed the advice of employer and employee representatives in a frank and friendly manner, and all of the participants in the work of the joint committee made contributions which sometimes constituted significant amendments to the original scheme of the legislation. To a large extent the manner of the statute's enactment as much as the merit of its substantive provisions gave hope that the Public Service Staff Relations Act would in fact prove workable. So far the predominant attitude of those engaged in administering the act and in representing the interest groups subject to its provisions seems to be one of good faith and a reasonable degree of self-restraint.

THE PUBLIC SERVICE STAFF RELATIONS ACT

Coverage

The Public Service Staff Relations Act applies to all employees in the public service of Canada, either in the central administration or in one of several autonomous agencies. The act defines the "employer" by reference to two lists, one of government departments and agencies forming part of the central administration and the other of autonomous agencies identified as "separate employers."[12] Within the central administration the Treasury Board performs the employer function; the separate employers either conduct their own labor relations or delegate that function to the Treasury Board. There seems to have been little rational basis for assigning a given agency to one or the other list of employers,[13] and it must be assumed that the two lists reflect established traditions or political sensitivities which caused some agencies to enjoy greater autonomy than others. It should also be noted that a number of government-owned corporations, such as the Canadian National Railway and Air Canada, fall under general federal labor relations legislation[14] rather than under the special public sector statute.

The Treasury Board is a committee of senior cabinet ministers, chaired by a president and with its own staff,[15] which represents its "client" agencies before the various tribunals established under the act, conducts labor negotiations, and monitors employment conditions and grievance-handling procedures at the departmental level. The Treasury Board, moreover, represents a tendency toward centralization, modernization, and professionalization of personnel management. Still, individual government departments and agencies—including those represented by the Treasury Board—tend to value their traditional autonomy and to cling to precollective bargaining habits of employer-employee relations.

To what extent these separate departmental foci of power can be displaced by the central staff of the Treasury Board is more than a mere practical or political problem. It also involves policy considerations as to whether, or to what extent, specialized needs and wishes of various branches of the public service should give way in the interest of general administrative uniformity. The potential for conflict created by this arrangement is obvious, and it would be more serious if it were not for the extreme delicacy shown by the Treasury Board staff in its relations with the "client" departments of government.[16]

Very few categories of public "employees" other than managerial personnel are denied the right of collective bargaining under the act,[17] and the statutory definition of managerial personnel is so narrow that the exception covers only a minimum number of persons.[18] In this connection it is important to emphasize that there existed in the Canadian public service a long-standing tradition linking managerial and nonmanagerial personnel together in various employee associations. The survival of this tradition in the face of the new statutory prohibition against management intervention in the affairs of employee associations may prove to be a matter of some controversy.[19] However, the situation is not without its parallels in the private sector, and it seems likely that over a period of time managerial and bargaining unit personnel will by a process of attrition become more clearly disassociated. The one area in which this process may be slow is among professional and scientific personnel, who are bound together by interests and qualifications which transcend the employment relationship.[20]

Administration

The act is administered by the Public Service Staff Relations Board (PSSRB), an independent administrative tribunal. In the common Canadian mode, the PSSRB is tripartite in composition, with two neutral presiding officers and an equal number of members "representative . . . of the interests of employees and of . . . the employer."[21] To ensure the neutral members' independence, they hold office for ten years and can be removed only by the procedure applicable to the removal of federal judges. The partisan members hold office for up to seven years, subject to removal by the cabinet "for cause."[22]

Both the Arbitration Tribunal, which deals with interest disputes,[23] and a corps of adjudicators, which deals with grievances,[24] operate under the administrative aegis of the PSSRB.[25] The board itself appoints members of the Arbitration Tribunal[26] and nominates its chairman for appointment by the federal cabinet;[27] the board also nominates adjudicators for appointment.[28] Moreover, the chairman of the PSSRB is empowered to appoint conciliators and expert or technical assistants.[29] The Preparatory Committee presumably devised these arrangements in order to strengthen the independence and impartiality of the board, and noted that the minister of labour could hardly be expected to assume administrative responsibility for such "third party" functions as conciliation, which normally are not performed by a labor relations board at all. Unlike the private sector, in public employment the government does not "stand between an employer and a group of organized employees in a position of impartiality. . . ."[30] Thus it can be fairly said that the administration of the act is almost completely free of the employer's control or influence.[31] The importance of this point for the "normalization" of employer-employee relations in the public sector can hardly be overemphasized. The Canadian arrangement is far more likely to win the confidence of public employees than the typical advisory body in the United States. Such bodies, often created by executive order, depend for their very existence on the grace and favor of the appointing power, and public employees, not surprisingly, may sometimes feel that their recommendations are not completely unbiased.

Not directly involved in the scheme of collective baragining, but very definitely a part of the environment of employer-employee relations at the federal level, is the Public Service Commission. This commission administers the Public Service Employment Act,[32] which establishes and implements the civil service or "merit" system of appointments and promotions, and provides a vehicle for employee training and development programs. This area of responsibility is much smaller than that exercised by the old Civil Service Commission prior to the advent of collective bargaining in the public sector. However,

there are still problems of delimiting the jurisdictional boundaries between the Public Service Commission and the other
bodies engaged in administering the collective bargaining relationship.

Protection of Basic Rights

The basic approach of the Preparatory Committee was to
seek normalization of industrial relations in the public service:

> Legislation governing industrial relations in the private
> sector usually contains a number of provisions designed to
> protect the integrity of the collective bargaining relation-
> ship, including: a declaration of the freedom of employees
> to belong to any organization of their choice; a prohibition
> of employer interference in the organization or administra-
> tion of any employee organization; and an assurance that
> employees may exercise their rights without threats, intim-
> idation or reprisals from agents of employee organizations
> or the employer.
>
> In the opinion of the Preparatory Committee, the prin-
> ciples underlying provisions of this kind are of fundamental
> importance and should be made to apply clearly to the
> Public Service system.[33]

The legislation, as finally enacted, reflects this basic philosophy of the Preparatory Committee. Freedom of association
is clearly proclaimed,[34] and interference with that freedom by
managerial personnel is clearly forbidden. In particular, prohibitions are announced against domination of unions,[35] discrimina-
tion in employment against unionists, and other analogous coercive tactics.[36] These prohibitions are made effective by a procedure for the laying of complaints against the employer
(i.e. the government) and any person acting on its behalf.[37]

The PSSRB is given jurisdiction to hear and determine
such complaints, to make remedial orders, and to invoke two
different sanctions to ensure compliance. The board may make
a report of noncompliance to Parliament[38] (which would no
doubt be extremely embarrassing for the government) or consent

to the prosecution of any individual who is guilty of a violation of the prohibitions contained in the act.[39] However, beyond the laying of a report before Parliament, no sanctions are directly available against the government itself. It is clear that conformity to the policy of the law ultimately depends on the government's willing compliance rather than the fear of sanctions. In any event, where isolated acts of antiunionism are most likely to occur (if at all) is at the lower echelons of management or at points geographically remote from the main administrative centers. No doubt the ability of the Treasury Board to assume control of such situations will lead to effective self-policing on the employer side, and corrective measures will be taken without the need to invoke the enforcement machinery of the statute. To date there have been few complaints of unfair labor practices, and the enforcement provisions of the act have not yet been invoked.

Establishing the Bargaining Relationship

The statute provides that certification must form the basis of all bargaining relationships.[40] In this respect the federal public service legislation differs to some extent from the private sector counterpart statutes, which permit voluntary recognition. However, the requirement that a bargaining agent be certified does avoid the risk that the employer will deal with a favored union which does not enjoy the support of a majority of its constituents.

In the period after the act first came into force, considerable controversy arose as to which employee organizations were eligible to obtain certification. The stakes were high, since disqualification would preclude an organization from participation in the rapid race to win bargaining rights for virtually the entire public service.

Illustrative of the problems raised are three cases. In contemplation of the new statute, several major public service employee associations had banded together to form the Public Service Alliance of Canada. In the *Hospital Services* case, the constitutionality of this coalition was challenged, and the validity of evidence of membership tendered by it was impugned. The PSSRB sustained the alliance on both counts, declining to evaluate the internal mechanisms by which the former organizations had agreed to merge, and accepting as evidence of continuing membership in the alliance dues checked off after the merger on the basis of premerger authorizations. An adverse ruling would have deprived one of the major intended beneficiaries of the act of the right to participate in the critical contests for initial certification rights. Second, in the *Ships' Crews* case it was argued that a union which comprised both civil servants and private sector employees was ineligible to obtain certification. It was contended that such a union might be responsive to the direction of persons who were not concerned with, and might be inimical to, the interests of the public service. The board also rejected this contention, finding in the legislative history no intention to grant a monopoly on representation rights to the old-line civil service associations. However, the board concluded with a warning that should it be found that extrinsic considerations were affecting its representation of public employees, the status of the union might be jeopardized. The third case, the *Council of Postal Unions* case, raised the fairly fundamental question of whether certification should be granted to a union which disenfranchised certain persons within the bargaining unit which it claimed to represent. Here the board drew the line, insisting that the price of certification was access to membership for all employees in the bargaining unit.[41] In the same case the board insisted that a newly formed council of unions be established according to constitutional processes which, at a minimum, included a clear undertaking by each of its constituent members to participate in collective bargaining through the medium of the council.

The statute does not explicitly set forth the method by which a union's majority status is to be demonstrated on an application for certification. However, the board has adopted a rule of thumb which accords certification outright to unions which can demonstrate a membership exceeding 52 percent of the employees in the bargaining unit, while unions which can demonstrate a substantial (but lesser) level of support must have their status tested by secret ballot vote. Parenthetically, it may be noted that the logistics of taking a vote present potentially staggering problems. How to conduct a ballot of ships' crews on a number of vessels which may be on the high seas for months at a time? Or of lighthouse keepers who are virtually inaccessible except by helicopter? In such difficult circumstances, problems of communication and of the integrity of the secret ballot have been met with considerable ingenuity by the board and with some degree of realism by the parties.

Upon certification, a bargaining agent becomes the exclusive representative of all employees in the bargaining unit for purposes of both negotiation and grievance handling.[42] The importation into the public service of this well-recognized private sector principle creates the necessity of defining the limits of the bargaining unit within which this exclusive right of representation prevails. Potentially this is an extremely difficult problem because of the unity of the management structure (at least in the central administration), and the need to preserve uniformity within the public service of employment conditions for persons performing analogous work. Centrifugal forces are also strong: geographic dispersion, the nationalist impulse among federal employees in Quebec, self-assertion of occupational groups afraid of being yoked with other groups thought to possess lesser bargaining power.

Rather than forcing the PSSRB to confront these problems during the hectic initial period when collective bargaining first was introduced into the public service, the legislation established a number of statutory bargaining units for the duration of the "initial certification period."[43] These statutory bargaining units reflect a new system of job classification which had been introduced by the Civil Service Commission in 1964. The central administration is divided into seventy-two occupational groups which, in turn, are clustered into five broad occupational categories established by the statute: scientific and professional, administrative and foreign service, technical, administrative support, and operational. During the initial certification period the board was obliged to adhere to these statutory bargaining units unless it determined "that such a bargaining unit would not permit satisfactory representation of employees . . . and . . . would not constitute a unit of employees appropriate for collective bargaining."[44] The only other contemplated departure from the statutorily defined bargaining units, at the initial stage, would require a decision by the board to divide an occupational group into separate supervisory and nonsupervisory bargaining units.

The initial certification period for each broad occupational category was designed to last for a period of approximately twenty months. Thereafter the PSSRB may redefine bargaining units, upon application, so long as the broad occupational categories established by the statute are kept discreet.[45] In recognition of the employer's interest in uniformity throughout the public service, however, the board is required to "have regard to" the nature of the established classification structure in any redefinition of bargaining units.[46]

Given the enormous tasks associated with bringing the legislation into operation, the idea of the initial certification period seems sound. While this arrangement may, to some extent, have inhibited employees in their desire to associate together for collective bargaining purposes, by imposing predetermined boundaries on the bargaining units, it did expedite the certification process and in the long run thereby strengthened the system of collective bargaining. Moreover, with experience under the statute during the initial certification period, the board is now able to go about its job of redefining units more intelligently, should that prove necessary.

As of March 31, 1970 (approximately three years after the enactment of the statute), virtually the entire federal public service has been organized. In the central administration, some eighty bargaining units have now been certified comprising approximately 190,000 employees; barely 2000 eligible employees in a potential maximum of five additional units remain unrepresented. An additional thirty-four "separate employer" units have been certified, comprising some 7000 employees.

Predictably, employee organizations with deep and distinctive traditions in the public service have been most successful in organizing and obtaining certification. The largest, the Public Service Alliance of Canada (PSAC), represents 133,000 employees in fifty-three units; the Professional Institute of the Public Service of Canada (PIPS) represents almost 13,000 employees in thirty-nine units; the Council of Postal Unions (CPU) is certified for that department's entire eligible staff of over 27,000 workers. Thus over 85 percent of the public service is represented by such organizations. The remaining 15 percent—approximately 24,000 employees—bargain through regular private-sector unions.

However, there is no suggestion that the distinctive public sector organizations are in any sense "tame" or "captive" groups, as compared with the private sector unions. As they have gained experience and overcome the initial problems of organization, they have increasingly exhibited a degree of sophistication and aggressiveness which bespeaks a high quality of representation for their constituents. Indeed, as will be seen, the postal unions are at least as aggressive as any in the country.

Resolving Impasses: Arbitration or Strike?

Upon timely notice being given, both the employer and the bargaining agent are required "to bargain collectively in good faith and make every reasonable effort to conclude a collective agreement."[47] As a reflection of the general adherence to private sector principles, this admonition is hardly surprising.

However, it is the procedure for resolving negotiation impasses which represents the most novel, perhaps the most radical, feature of the statute. Following certification, a bargaining agent is required to specify "which . . . shall be the process for resolution of any dispute to which it may be a party . . . ,"[48] the alternatives being referral to arbitration or referral to a conciliation board.[49] Since arbitral awards are "binding on the employer and the bargaining agent . . . and on the employees,"[50] it is obvious that specification of arbitration forecloses the possibility of a strike.[51] However, no comparable binding effect is assigned to the report of a conciliation board, and no prohibitions exist anywhere in the statute which would preclude a post-conciliation strike. By inference, then, strikes are permitted following exhaustion of the conciliation process.

The failure to announce affirmatively the existence of a right to strike is hardly surprising. On the one hand, Canadian labor relations statutes typically do not contain an express reference to such a right, although the courts have recognized that a common law right to strike is assumed and adopted by such legislation.[52] On the other hand, there had never been a clear statement that strikes of public servants were per se illegal,[53] so that there was no need to reverse an existing legal norm.

In permitting bargaining agents to resort to strikes, the statute does not entirely abandon the public interest in the continued operation of government to the whimsy of negotiators. If a union has elected to resolve its collective bargaining impasses by strike rather than arbitration, certain employees within the bargaining unit (referred to in the statute as "designated employees") are forbidden to strike if their duties "consist in whole or in part of duties, the performance of which at any particular time or after any specified period of time is or will be necessary in the interest of the safety or security of the public."[54]

It should be noted, first, that the definition of "designated employees" is tightly circumscribed. The right to strike is denied only to persons whose absence from work would imperil interests which are absolutely vital. There is no open-ended language referring to "public interest" or "convenience" or "welfare." Second, the designated employees alone are precluded from striking, but all other employees in the bargaining unit are free to do so. Since the designated employees receive the benefit of any collective agreement negotiated by their bargaining agent, even they continue to benefit, albeit vicariously, from any economic power generated by the actual or threatened exercise of the strike option. Third, the procedure by which designated employees are to be identified is designed to avoid controversy during the course of a strike. Within twenty days after notice to bargain has been served by either party, the employer is required to establish a list of designated employees. If no objection is taken to the employer's list, all of the persons so identified are taken to be "designated." However, in the event that an objection is made by the bargaining agent, the board holds a hearing and determines the issue.

In fact, the parties have been largely able to agree upon the identification of designated employees. Contrary to some fears expressed prior to the enactment of the statute, the device has not been promiscuously used in order to withdraw the right to strike from employees upon whom it was statutorily conferred. As of March 31, 1970, some 37,725 employees were included in units which had opted for the strike; of these only 2700 were designated employees—about 7.5 percent.

On the other hand, postal workers comprise 27,500 of these employees, and none of them are designated. Of the remaining 10,000, then, about 25 percent are designated. While this might seem like a more significant impairment of the potential economic impact of a strike, in only a single instance (of the fourteen units involved) was the PSSRB called upon to decide which employees fell within the statutory definition; in all other cases the parties were able to agree.

In the *Electronics Group* case, the employees whose designation was challenged were electronics technicians engaged in the maintenance of air and maritime navigational aids.[55] In essence, the board ruled that all employees involved in servicing integrated systems which might possibly be required by ships or planes in distress would be designated, but on a "standby" basis. The effect of the decision was to permit the employer to call in for work—when needed, but not on a regular basis—employees required to keep all navigational aid systems in full working order. However, the decision does not clearly indicate whether, within the limits of the facilities available, the employer would be free to "carry on business as usual," in the sense of attempting to accommodate the normal flow of commercial air and sea traffic. One employee-nominated board member dissented on this point.

More important than the facts of the particular case is

the board's adumbration of the definition of "designated employees" and the policy implications of this definition:

Persons who are engaged in the functions defined in section 79(1) of the Act are not permitted to strike at any time (see section 101(1)(c)). It is not that collective bargaining rights are denied to such persons. The subsidiary principle recognized by the Act is that one of the collective bargaining rights that may normally be exercised by employees cannot be exercised by specified persons if its exercise would jeopardize public safety and security as distinct from interfering with the capacity of the employer—as an employer—to carry on its day-to-day business. The role of the strike in North America is generally accepted to be purely economic. The traditional and normal raison d'etre of a strike is to interfere with, or bring to a stop, the normal operations of the employer—as an employer—with a view to reducing the employer's bargaining power and increasing that of the employees. The strike has been tolerated, accepted and even encouraged by society itself as a means of balancing the bargaining power of the employer and the employees with a view to an eventual settlement. By-products of the strike are the inconvenience or hardship that may be suffered by the employer's customers. But the prime target is the employer, not the public. If the exercise of the right to strike does affect the safety and security of the public, rather than the profitability or convenience of the employer, the role of the strike is transformed by a change in kind and not merely a change of degree or effectiveness.

The Act does not draw the line at "convenience of the public" but at "safety or security of the public." This does not mean that the public would always necessarily suffer if the employees to whom the section applies withdraw their services. It does mean that where there are reasonable grounds for accepting the *probability*, or even perhaps only a *possibility*, that human life or public safety and security would suffer, section 79(1) comes into play.

The statute does not appear to provide expressly for the designation of additional employees during the strike, in the event that the employer, or the board, has misjudged the numbers and types of employees required to protect the public interest. However, as it stated in the *Electronics Group* case, there is no doubt that the PSSRB would mobilize its full statutory resources to cope with such a crisis, including its power to "review, rescind, amend, alter or vary any decision or order made by it."[56] It is at least arguable, of course, that the employer and the board should have anticipated all contingencies in making the original designations. However, were the board precluded from reexamining the problem (at least in the light of subsequent developments), the employer might be prompted to enlarge greatly the numbers of designated employees on the basis of remote and hypothetical contingencies.[57] This would hardly facilitate the full exercise of the rights conferred by the statute.

A second series of potential problems is posed by the relationship between striking employees and designated employees in the same bargaining unit. Suppose that the employer requires that a skeleton staff remain on duty during a strike: how are individuals within a category of designated employees to be identified for such work? What of illness or resignation by designated employees? Are the same individuals to work throughout the strike? Or are the strikers to serve in rotation? What of the risk of slowdown or work-to-rule by designated employees? And what of the wages paid to designated employees: to the extent that they exceed strike pay, should the surplus be turned over to the union strike fund? All of these questions remain unanswered after the first strike under the act, because no designated employees were involved in the unit in which it occurred. Because of its peculiar facts, and because the board was not dealing with an actual strike situation, the *Electronics Group* case likewise offers little guidance on these matters.

Yet conceding that these questions are potentially troublesome, the statutory procedure for designating employees in advance of an actual strike situation is fundamentally sound.

The fact that the parties are not locked in conflict enhances the chance that they will agree to the list of designated employees. If they do not agree, the difficult adjudicative problems of defining and identifying such persons can be undertaken without undue pressure. Finally, if a large proportion of employees in the unit is to be designated, so that the union's ability to strike would be seriously impaired, this fact can be made obvious at an early stage in the proceedings so that the union can opt for arbitration instead.

As a corollary to the proposition that employees should be permitted to select the strike option if they wish, the statute is designed to induce them not to take that option by offering them attractive alternatives. Several institutional arrangements are provided which undoubtedly contribute to the amicable settlement of disputes.

Perhaps most important in this regard is the provision of a factual framework for enlightened bargaining. The Pay Research Bureau, established in 1957, is an independent agency operating under the administrative aegis of the chairman of the PSSRB.[58] As its name implies, the function of the bureau is to gather and disseminate factual, objective, and impartial data relating to wages and employment conditions in the public service. Its work, considered to be of a very high standard, is guided by bipartisan technical consultation with the government and the employee associations. Data produced by the bureau is, of course, equally accessible to both sides.

Relying on both mailed surveys and field studies, the bureau has necessarily sought, and apparently received, the cooperation of private sector employers with whom comparisons must necessarily be made. Ironically, the very success of the bureau in gathering and analyzing data has generated pressures upon it to make the results of its research available to private industry and, presumably, unions. So far these pressures have been resisted, to a large degree, because the bureau's raison d'etre is to serve the public sector and because wider distribution and use of its reports might involve a greater risk of controversy than the bureau has hitherto had to run.[59]

In the public sector there can be little doubt: the bureau

has materially assisted the progress of negotiations, although it plays no direct role in wage determination beyond providing data to both sides. By largely removing factual issues from the realm of controversy, the bureau permits negotiators to focus attention on the admittedly difficult tasks of choosing criteria by which those facts are to be measured and of developing arguments to present to the opposite party, the Arbitration Tribunal, or a conciliation board (when a strike is in contemplation).

Second, if the parties fail to resolve their differences in direct negotiation, the dispute does not pass directly to arbitration or strike. Provision is made for the intervention of a conciliator on the request of either party.[60] Only if he fails to bring the parties together does the focus shift from bargaining to more authoritative forms of third-party intervention.

In the case of bargaining units eligible to strike, the chairman of the PSSRB, on his own initiative or on the application of either party, may appoint a three-man conciliation board charged with the obligation to "endeavour to bring about agreement between the parties."[61] Failing in this effort, the board reports its findings and recommendations to the chairman, who may then publish the report. While the conciliation board report is not binding, its publication (especially if unanimous) is intended to generate public pressure upon the parties for acceptance. Whether such pressure is in fact generated at all, or is effective, is a matter of conjecture. However, both the mediative and fact-finding functions of the conciliation board are potentially useful.

In the case of arbitration-bound units, when the time for arbitration finally arrives, elaborate provision is made for the clear definition of issues. The Arbitration Tribunal, moreover, is not simply left to speculate at large upon the principles by which public employment working conditions are to be fixed. The statute provides the Arbitration Tribunal—and presumably negotiators seeking to avoid arbitration—with criteria for determining wages and working conditions.[62] While these criteria are admittedly broad, they at least constitute an attempt by Parliament to discharge its obligations by stating that public employees are to enjoy conditions of employment comparable to those in the private sector. Coupled with the data generated by the Pay Research Bureau and submitted to the scrutiny of an Arbitration Tribunal staffed by men of high competence, these legislative guidelines are likely to produce a decision which will be respected. Arbitration, then, is not likely to be feared by either side as involving risks of irresponsible or ill-informed third-party decision-making. On the other hand, the very rationality of the arbitral process may enable the parties to simulate, and thus avoid, it.

One feature of the awards of the Arbitration Tribunal may seem odd to those who view a reasoned judgment as the hallmark of adjudication. In all four cases it has heard thus far, the tribunal has chosen simply to announce its award on the matters at issue without articulating reasons. The statute does prohibit dissident members of the tribunal from issuing separate awards or comments on the majority (or chairman's) award,[63] but it would not appear to preclude exposition by the chairman of the considerations which produced his authoritative decision. Perhaps this practice reflects a desire to avoid creating an atmosphere of legalism, or to preserve sufficient uncertainty in decision-making so that the parties will wish to settle rather than chance an unpredictable award.

So far, then, as attractive alternatives to the strike could be devised, this seems to have been done in the Public Service Staff Relations Act. Have the arrangements described above either induced employees to opt for arbitration rather than conciliation-strike or to stop short of strike action, although it is legally available in a particular situation?

As of March 31, 1970, all 114 bargaining units had elected between arbitration and conciliation-strike. Only 14 units, containing approximately 37,000 employees, have turned their backs on arbitration, and all but some 10,000 of these employees are the militant postal workers. The balance of almost 160,000 employees in 100 bargaining units have voluntarily relinquished the right to strike—surely evidence of their desire to avoid disruption of public services, if at all possible.

The vital question is whether these decisions, taken in

the relatively euphoric period following the enactment of the statute, will be regretted and repudiated in the light of experience. To date, no unit has exercised its right to change its election. However, if significant discrepancies were believed to exist in favor of units which had "gone the strike route," or if arbitration-bound units came to lose confidence in the collective bargaining process, such changes of election would rapidly occur.

The Collective Bargaining System in Operation

Thus far actual experience under each system has been relatively satisfactory. It has been conventionally held that parties who do not confront the possibility of a strike will seldom compromise their differences, preferring to take their chances with an arbitrator rather than conclude an agreement through direct negotiations. At least to a limited extent, however, experience under the Public Service Staff Relations Act suggests that arbitration does not necessarily spell the end of real collective bargaining. Agreements have been signed in almost all bargaining units governed by the arbitration option. Of these, over 70 percent were the product of direct negotiations, unassisted even by a conciliator. The Arbitration Tribunal has had to decide only four controversies out of a potential of almost one hundred cases.

Nor has the choice of the right to strike in fourteen units led to excessive strife. As of March 31, 1970, first agreements had been signed in eleven units and negotiations were underway in the remaining three. Of these eleven agreements, five were concluded in direct negotiations, six after the intervention of a conciliation board, and only one—in the post office—was the product of an actual strike.

In summary, then, to the extent that the efficacy of either system is to be tested by its ability to generate collective agreements without recourse either to strike or arbitration, the results have been quite satisfactory.

To be sure, there are several unusual circumstances which may have contributed to the unexpectedly good record in arbitration-bound units. First, it must be remembered that the unions concerned had voluntarily abandoned their right to strike. It could be assumed, therefore, that they had decided to approach collective bargaining in a more responsible, less militant, posture than either their private sector or strike-potential public sector brethren. Second, the government is obviously aware of the risk that disillusion with bargaining under the arbitration option might lead to a massive drift toward the strike option. Accordingly, it is reasonable to assume that the government's bargaining stance has been designed to avoid any invidious distinctions.

Moreover, if attention is focused on certain of the strains and defects in the bargaining process, particularly as these are perceived by the participants, the picture is somewhat less idyllic than the percentage of successful negotiations would suggest.

The concluding section of this chapter is devoted to an analysis of collective bargaining in the post office, which has been the source of the most intractable problems in the entire system. However, it is also useful to canvass, at least in general terms, the relationship between other groups in the system—principally the Treasury Board and the Public Service Alliance of Canada (PSAC), whose bargaining relationship embraces almost two thirds of the employees covered by the statute.[64]

To begin with an analysis of the principal participants, it seems evident that neither has yet evolved wholly satisfactory institutional structures necessary to discharge its bargaining functions with maximum efficiency.

The PSAC is, in effect, a centralized organization with administrative "components" organized along departmental lines. Since the statutory bargaining units stretch "horizontally" along occupational lines, and across departmental lines, the PSAC itself (rather than its components) must possess the authority and responsibility for negotiations. Nonetheless, geographical dispersion and day-to-day work contacts tend to produce some contrary pressures for departmental or "component" loyalties. For example, civilian employees in different occupational categories at an armed forces base remote from other government operations may tend to identify with each other through the local organization of the Union of National Defense Employees more than they identify with other employees in the same occupational group—and bargaining unit—working in Ottawa for another department. Moreover, the ever present risk of disaffection by Quebec-based federal employees poses a further threat to centralized PSAC authority. Finally, as in any large labor organization, the PSAC must reconcile the varying degrees of sophistication and militancy among its members.

To date the PSAC leadership has recognized the risks inherent in these centrifugal forces[65] and has moved effectively to overcome them where possible. As the PSAC staffing and servicing problems produced by rapid growth are slowly resolved, and the organization is better able to perform the functions it has undertaken, local foci of discontent are likely to disappear.

The Treasury Board's problems would appear to be more difficult. As indicated, the Treasury Board is a permanent cabinet committee, presided over by a senior minister—the president of the Treasury Board—and permanently staffed to perform its varied functions in overseeing the organization, programs, and expenditures of the federal government.

In formulating the government's bargaining position in relation to forthcoming negotiations, the Compensation and Conditions Division of the Treasury Board develops data and recommends terms which are thought to be reasonable. These are discussed with the director of the Staff Relations Division and the assistant secretary of the Personnel Policy Branch, under whom both divisions operate. A proposal is then placed before a special cabinet committee which overlaps, but is not coterminous with, the Treasury Board ministers. This cabinet committee defines the mandate which will be given to the negotiating team, and must likewise redefine the mandate should settlement within its terms prove impossible. The negotiating team is usually headed by a Treasury Board official and comprises as well representation from the departments most affected by the negotiations.

As will be obvious even from this oversimplified exposition, the formulation of the employer's initial position, its modification during negotiations, and ultimate approval of any settlement all require the participation of a variety of Treasury Board, cabinet, and departmental interests. This participation is time-consuming and, moreover, may reflect different motivations and attitudes. It can be postulated, for example, that the cabinet committee's primary concern might be the total cost of a settlement proposal; the Treasury Board's concern might be the likelihood of the proposal being accepted by the other side or its effect on other negotiations in the future; while the departments might be most concerned about the impact of a proposal on its ability to perform its functions effectively.

A further complicating factor, which perhaps will ease over time, relates to a difference in "style" between Treasury Board and departmental representatives. The advent of collective bargaining in the federal public service created a demand for trained negotiators and other labor relations and personnel specialists. Because this need could not be met by intramural recruitment, the Treasury Board hired a number of experienced private sector experts. Their attitudes appear to have differed markedly from the traditional, more paternalistic departmental officials with whom the PSAC had formerly dealt. However, by a process of rotation, training, and informal socialization, these differences in attitude are being slowly erased.

The net burden of these considerations in the eyes of the employee organizations is that negotiations are unduly prolonged and controversies unnecessarily exacerbated. Special criticism is levied at the Treasury Board's alleged preoccupation with definitions and other items of contract language, its failure to deal rapidly with minor issues, and, above all, the lack of authority vested in its negotiating team. Estimates of the number of levels through which decisions about comparatively minor issues have to pass between negotiators and the cabinet committee vary from three to five. One spokesman stated, "It's like bargaining with ghosts." PSAC president Edwards has been quoted as stating that the positions adopted by the Treasury Board "would be considered ludicrous by anyone knowledgeable about industrial relations," and Mr. Barnes, the executive director of the professional employees association, PIPS, has stated: "The Treasury Board seems bent on eroding and destroying such limited stocks of confidence and respect as may have remained as the residue of the previous systems of staff relations. . . . [There is] scant evidence of any attempt to build the foundations of a relationship based on confidence and respect."[66] The PSAC at one point went so far as to state that unless the Treasury Board was prepared to carry out "realistic bargaining," it would end all current negotiations and refer all issues to arbitration.

These charges are, of course, denied by the Treasury Board, which claims that any delays are not the product of structural defects but are rather inherent in the establishment of any new regime of employment relations. According to the Treasury Board, even important issues can be speedily determined by the cabinet committee when, in fact, there is an imminent prospect of settlement. Moreover, it has been suggested by way of countercharge that the unions are anxious to keep open the possibility of direct, old-style contact with the cabinet over the heads of Treasury Board negotiators, so that they can obtain through political lobbying what they fail to win through genuine collective bargaining. Whatever the truth of the matter, it is clear that delays are considerable and that union frustrations are genuine. These facts do create stresses upon the system.

Two additional constraints are, in the long run, more significant than the structural organization of the parties: the problems of the statutory scope of negotiations and of the relationship between the government's collective bargaining stance as an employer and its commitment to antiinflationary measures in managing the national economy.

Turning first to the statutory scope of negotiations, the Report of the Preparatory Committee had clearly recommended "that legislation place no limitation on the subject-matter of discussion at the bargaining table."[67] However, it had also proposed that arbitration (the only method of dispute settlement contemplated) be limited to controversies over rates of pay, standard hours of work, leave entitlement, and directly related conditions of employment. The Preparatory Committee stated its firm views as to the exclusion of certain topics from arbitration: "The entitlement of employees to superannuation, death benefit and accident compensation should continue to be governed by law. Furthermore, it should be made clear that the subject-matter of arbitration may in no circumstance extend to the processes governing appointment, transfer, promotion, demotion, lay-off, discharge, discipline and classification."[68] This attempt to permit negotiation while withholding the means of dispute resolution may prove to be a source of difficulty, especially since arbitration was coupled with the strike option in the final version of the statute. A union denied satisfaction on one of the "excluded" matters may simply become intransigent over those which fall within the "negotiable" category. Even where the union has opted for arbitration rather than strike, such frustration would necessarily impair prearbitration bargaining.

Nonetheless, the statute expressly prohibits the making of an agreement, a conciliation board report, or an arbitral award which would require the enactment of legislation, other than for the purpose of appropriating funds, or which would detract from the operation of the other statutes enacted as part of the comprehensive scheme for public service employment relations.[69] In the case of agreements voluntarily concluded, or concluded as the result of a strike, any other type of provision is presumably to be permitted. The statutory duty to bargain "with a view to the conclusion . . . of a collective agreement"[70] seems to extend to all provisions falling with the statutory definition of a collective agreement: "provisions respecting terms and conditions of employment and related matters."[71] However, the power of the Arbitration Tribunal to make an award in the event the parties fail to make an agreement is much more carefully circumscribed: "an arbitral award may deal with rates of pay, hours of work, leave entitlement, standards of discipline and other terms and conditions of employment *directly related thereto*."[72] In several awards the Arbitration Tribunal has indicated that it attaches great importance to the concluding words and has held, for example, that proposals relating to job security or grievance procedure could not form part of an award, since they were not "directly related to" the matters specifically enumerated in the act.

But whether it relates to an agreement or an award, the prohibition against detracting from the operation of other statutes is a very serious problem indeed. In effect this prohibition seeks to avoid the possibility of a clash between the new collective bargaining regime and the older civil service system, but does so in favor of the old at the expense of the new.

The Public Service Staff Relations Act prohibits the making of an arbitral award or a conciliation board report dealing with "the standards, procedures or processes governing the appointment, . . . demotion, transfer, lay-off or release" of employees.[73] The Public Service Employment Act confers upon the Public Service Commission "the exclusive right and authority to make appointments,"[74] as well as a mandate to "establish the merit of candidates" for appointment,"[75] and to oversee the processes of promotion, demotion, and layoff.[76] Other statutes place beyond the reach of collective negotiation such important job rights as pensions. But it is almost inevitable that unions will seek to influence the determination of standards governing these important incidents of employment, particularly in relation to job security. Would a strike aimed at such objectives be unlawful? Even if it were, will not the existence of a deeply felt concern ultimately require a vehicle for its amicable resolution? Will not the absence of such a vehicle haunt the collective bargaining process?

No mechanism is provided for easing possible tensions between the civil service system and the collective bargaining system, except that the commission is required "from time to time [to] consult with representatives of any employee organization certified as a bargaining agent . . . or with the employer . . . with respect to the selection standards . . . or the principles governing the appraisal [and] promotion . . . of employees."[77] This admonition is hardly a substitute for a formal system of bargaining in relation to matters falling within the jurisdiction of the commission. It does nothing at all to facilitate resolution of other issues regulated by different statutes.

Finally, a general provision of the Public Service Staff Relations Act authorizes the government, by cabinet order, to conclusively claim immunity from doing anything contrary to the "safety or security of Canada or any state allied or associated with Canada."[78] In practice this limitation is unlikely to present significant problems.

The other major irritant in the bargaining relationships between the federal government and organizations of its employees is the war against inflation. This affects negotiations in two ways.

First, the government is anxious to promote efficiency and hold down expense because of the increased costs of nonwage items associated with general inflationary trends throughout the economy, and because those same trends necessarily produce political pressure for higher levels of welfare benefits which also come out of the same limited budget as wage increases.

Second, as the country's most prominent, perhaps largest employer, the example set by government in negotiations with its own employees will have an important impact on the bargaining stance of private sector employers and unions. If the federal government yields increases which seem unduly large, they will be cited as precedents for similar private sector settlements. If, on the other hand, the federal government manages to hold the line, or at least to conform to the guidelines it proposes for the national economy, it may be in a better position to exact restraint from others.

Yet from the employees' point of view, government tough-mindedness must seem particularly unfair. First, government employees, like all workers, are forced to seek higher wages simply to retain equivalent buying power. Second, some groups in the public sector may be able to demonstrate historic injustices which, they may rightly claim, should be corrected— here the argument is that they should not be forced to continue to subsidize government functions by accepting unjustifiably low wages. Third, because of restrictions on the scope of bargaining, described above, government has a very limited range of nonmonetary concessions it can offer in lieu of wage increases. Finally, a hold-the-line policy on wages coming at the very outset of the era of collective bargaining makes for a particularly galling juxtaposition of harsh realities and unrealistic expectations. So much must have been expected from the new statute; so little must sometime seem to have been forthcoming.

One concluding observation must be recorded in any fair evaluation of the operation of the new system: there is no desire on the part of either party to turn the clock back. With all of its defects, the system is now accepted and promises in the long run to be adequate to the tasks it is called upon to perform. Perhaps the litmus test of this prediction is the extent to which it has succeeded in the most difficult area of all: the postal service. This will be examined in the concluding section of this chapter.

Implementation and Administration of Collective Agreements Grievances

Whether a collective agreement is the product of negotiation or of an arbitral award, it is binding upon the employer, the bargaining agent, and the employees in the bargaining unit.[79] In one short passage, the Preparatory Committee brushed aside both the practical and philosophical objections to such a provision:

> [In] many areas, the traditional authority of the Crown has been circumscribed by laws that limit its freedom of action or require its action to be brought to the attention of Parliament. The conclusion to which we have come can be simply stated: although the arbitration of disputes represents a limitation on the historic right of the Crown to determine unilaterally the terms and conditions of employment of those in its service, it is not likely to interfere with the capacity of the Government to discharge its responsibility.[80]

That the senior civil servants who constituted the committee should give such short shrift to the prerogatives asserted by their predecessors in office and their confreres in other jurisdictions is evidence of both their candor and their courage.

To be sure, there is still the overriding proviso that implementation is to be "subject to the appropriation by or under the authority of Parliament of any moneys that may be required by the employer therefor."[81] Nonetheless, the statute clearly assumes that Parliament will routinely honor agreements and awards while acknowledging the constitutional impossibility of avoiding ultimate legislative control of the public purse. Since the executive must reflect the majority party in the House of Commons and, as a practical matter, commands a majority vote on all issues, there is little likelihood that this statutory assumption will prove to be ill-founded.

In order to facilitate implementation, at least for the initial round of bargaining, a statutory timetable was established which provided that the first agreements negotiated in all bargaining units in each occupational category would all expire on a specified date.[82] Combined with a statutory stipulation that collective agreements could only be signed after a specified date[83] and for a minimum term of one year,[84] this provision was intended to bring the first (and, it is hoped, subsequent) agreements into a regular cycle of periodic pay revisions for the whole public service.

The obvious desirability of such a well-modulated arrangement, however, collided with the imponderables of a collective bargaining system: delays in certification due to union rivalry or simply to inexperience in organizing; delays in bargaining due to intraunion political processes, overwork of the employer representatives, and the predictable failure of negotiators to agree promptly on all issues outstanding. Thus, to cite but one example, the 1968 postal strike was settled less than two months before the date fixed by law for the expiry of the first collective agreements. While the minimum statutory term of one year could be satisfied by making this agreement retroactive, raw memories of the strike made the prospect of an immediate fresh round of negotiations too awful to contemplate. The parties ingeniously agreed, therefore, that two agreements should be signed, one operating retroactively and expiring on the date specified by the act, the other coming into effect and operating from that date forward.

With the wisdom of hindsight, it seems clear that a more flexible statutory timetable should have been established. However, the timing of representation questions—certification of new bargaining agents, severance of bargaining units, decertification—is fixed by reference to the expiry dates of the initial agreements.[85] Thus to have allowed a more protracted period for the first round of negotiations would have postponed for a further period the exercise by minority and dissident groups of their rights to select new bargaining agents.

Turning to the question of grievances, the provisions of the legislation are indeed liberal. An aggrieved employee may present a grievance concerning the effect upon himself of unilateral employer action relating to employment, or of a collective agreement or arbitral award, or of "any occurrence or matter affecting his terms and conditions of employment."[86] However, this broad-gauge grievance process is apparently designed for catharsis rather than confrontation. The employee cannot pursue his grievance to adjudication, unless it involves "the interpretation or application in respect of him of a provision of a collective agreement or an arbitral award, or . . . disciplinary action resulting in discharge, suspension or a financial penalty."[87] In all other cases the grievance can be pursued only through discussions with successively higher levels of management, up to but not including the minister responsible.

The statutory provisions for grievance processing in several respects might well be emulated in the private sector. First, the right to pursue grievances, as has been noted, is not delimited by the collective agreement alone. Thus the opportunity exists for an employee to bring to the attention of senior management sources of friction or incidents of maladministration by lower level officials. Second, the right to seek adjudication of grievances in the critical area of discipline is statute-based rather than contractual and extends to all employees, whether or not they are covered by a collective agreement and whether or not they are even eligible for inclusion in a bargaining unit.[88] Third, a balance is carefully struck between individual and group interests. An individual employee "owns" his personal grievance, but he may not challenge the interpretation or application of a collective agreement or arbitral award unless he has the approval and assistance of his union.[89] Since the interpretation of the collective agreement might set a precedent which would affect the entire bargaining unit, the certified bargaining agent retains exclusive control over such grievances (except in relation to discipline) by monitoring individual claims. If no bargaining agent is certified, of course the employee may seek representation by the union of his personal preference. Provision is also made for the filing of grievances by either party to the agreement, where the matter is not one which may be the subject of a grievance by an individual.[90]

Adjudication of grievances is the task of a corps of "adjudicators," one of whom, as chief adjudicator, assumes responsibility for the administration of the system. Adjudicators hold office for fixed terms and are assigned to individual cases as they arise.[91] Provision is also made for adjudication by a tripartite board[92] or by an adjudicator named in a collective agreement by the parties,[93] but both of these alternative devices are dependent upon the consent of both parties. To date neither has been resorted to. While there is much to be said for the naming of an adjudicator in an agreement (or, indeed, on an ad hoc basis by mutual designation of the parties), two considerations have militated against such a system. First, there is the obvious desire to preserve uniformity of decision throughout the public service in relation both to noncontractual matters and to like provisions of the numerous agreements.[94] Second, prior to the enactment of the new law, government employees had enjoyed a form of grievance appeal, the costs of which were borne by the public. This system has been carried forward and the parties do not now bear the costs of adjudication, unless they have elected to name their own adjudicator rather than accept one provided under the act.[95] Financial incentives thus encourage the use of the regular adjudicators.

Surprisingly, the first year under the new legislative scheme yielded barely 40 grievances for adjudication, and of these about half were held to be nonjusticiable on procedural or jurisdictional grounds. This initial paucity of cases reflected to some extent the preoccupation of the parties with the processes of certification and negotiation, to some extent their desire to be reasonable during the difficult period of adjustment to the new regime, and to some extent the absence of collective agreements which would provide a source both of new employee rights and of interpretative difficulties.

Each of these inhibitions on the volume of grievances has now fallen away, and the caseload has increased sharply. Over 240 cases were adjudicated during the first three years of the statute's operation. While the number is still relatively small, considering the numbers of employees involved, there is some evidence to suggest that it will continue to increase. The issues, of course, parallel those found in the private sector, except for matters which are nonnegotiable, and hence nonjusticiable, as a result of the statutory limitations on the scope of bargaining, outlined above.

While each adjudicator will no doubt contribute to the ethos of decision-making, an early decision suggested, as well, strong parallels between public sector adjudication and private sector grievance arbitration.

> The whole spirit and intent of the Public Service Staff Relations Act is to secure to the governmental employees covered by it . . . a regime of fair dealing which reflects concepts of industrial justice as they have developed in the private sector. To be sure, these concepts are expressed through institutions and rules which give due weight to the special characteristics of public employment. But the underlying principles of the new statute are to be taken as the expression of this aspiration, rather than as the haggard reflection of past policies.[96]

To complete this description of the institutional setting of grievance adjudication, it should be recorded that the decisions of an adjudicator are binding[97] and may be enforced[98] or reviewed only by the PSSRB.[99] Court review is precluded.[100] Finally, as has been indicated, certain matters fall within the purview of the Public Service Commission and thus cannot be made the subject either of a grievance or of adjudication.[101]

COLLECTIVE BARGAINING IN THE POSTAL SERVICE

Postal Employee Organizations

Traditionally, postal employees have regarded themselves as being quite distinct and separate from the main body of public servants. As noted, they were the first of the federal public employee groups to organize, in the 1880s, and remain today the most militant group, much closer to the ethos of industrial unionism in the private sector than to that of other public service organizations. Yet postal employees are in fact and in law government functionaries. Their self-image and allegiance to the norms of private sector unionism thus collide with the reality that they are but one of many government departments. This is a source of much frustration to the postal unions, and goes far to explain the distinctive posture adopted by them toward the Public Service Staff Relations Act.

Post office employees, uniquely among the more significant groups of government employees, have some history of militancy. In 1918 and again in 1924 they went on strike, on the latter occasion for twelve days. From that time to the present there has been an active cadre of unionist postal employees which has advocated and promoted an identification with the mainstream of the labor movement. While this group's importance can easily be overstressed, a long tradition of unionism has been one factor in detaching the postal employees from other civil servants. Its effect is particularly noticeable in certain urban centers in which private sector industrial unionism has been strong. Thus while union militancy did not surface in the post office generally until 1965, when it did arrive, it had some nucleus from which to expand.

A second distinctive characteristic of post office employment stems from the nature of the work performed. Postal workers constitute the largest aggregation of blue-collar, operational workers in government service. This sets them apart, in attitudes as well as functions, from the typical white-collar, clerical or technical public employee.

Third, while various measures had been taken, especially since the Second World War, to modernize the physical facilities, administration, and personnel policies of the civil service generally, the post office had been neglected to a large degree. Thus any improvements in morale (and efficiency) which might have provided a basis for constructive labor-management relationships elsewhere in the civil service were peculiarly lacking in the post office.

Each of these themes will be explored in the following pages; suffice to say, initially, that the post office is not a department like any other.

The post office's operating employees are divided into two major groups, each of which was organized by a separate union. The "inside workers" are those employees who receive, sort, and forward the mail, who staff the post office wickets, who dispatch and unload mail bags, and who operate postal vehicles. They are represented by the Canadian Union of Postal Workers (CUPW), whose 14,000 members comprise about 95 percent of those eligible to join. The second group, the "outside workers," make the final preparation of mail for delivery and actually deliver it from door to door; approximately 98 percent of these 11,300 letter carriers belong to the Letter Carriers Union of Canada (LCUC). Small groups of employees belong to other organizations, but they have not been significant in the recent history of labor relations in the post office.

For specific objectives, the two major unions had in recent years entered into alliances with each other, and often with the small 400-member Canadian Railway Mail Clerks' Federation (RMC). Finally, in 1965 the RMC and the two larger unions formed the Postal Workers' Brotherhood to represent all postal employees in negotiations. However, because the RMC demanded a voice which the other two unions considered disproportionate to its numbers, the coalition was dissolved.[102] The two large unions then formed a joint council, the Council of Postal Unions (CPU), which was certified under the Public

Service Staff Relations Act as the bargaining agent for the entire postal operations group on January 4, 1968. Excluded from the CPU bargaining unit were supervisors, part-time workers (defined as those who work 30 hours or less per week but on a regular basis), and railway mail clerks. The railway mail clerks subsequently joined the Public Service Alliance; in mid-1969 the CPU was certified for a bargaining unit comprising the part-time workers.

The CPU was conceived, at least in part, as a transitional step on the path to a complete merger between the letter carriers and the postal workers. So far the final steps have yet to be taken; in 1967 the projected merger date was 1969, but it has not come about. A merger would give the postal employees' union a financial base sufficiently large to support a professional staff and would eliminate the existing duplication in field services. At present each union employs nine or ten field officers, all of whom have their background in the postal service; neither union employs a professional whose background is not in the post office; neither union can afford a strike fund. Occasional professional and technical assistance is provided by the Canadian Labour Congress (with which both unions are affiliated) and some modest financial aid in time of need is contributed by local labor councils. Union of the two groups seems logically desirable but at present appears unlikely. The organizational problems associated with merger (such as integration of seniority lists) have not been solved, and the letter carriers fear domination by the more numerous postal workers. Even the present alliance between the two unions is an uneasy one. Moreover, the leadership of the unions, especially that of the LCUC, exercises at best a tenuous control over the rank and file. Fear of rank and file insurgency makes merger difficult and inhibits prompt implementation of decisions reached between the unions and the post office itself.

Before turning the coin to look at the post office department, it should be noted that emphasis upon the nonsupervisory operating employees has obscured the existence of another large group of post office employees—those not engaged in postal operations. These employees are members of organizations and bargaining units which stretch horizontally across the total structure of government employment. Post office staff relations with the "nonoperating" employees have been comparatively harmonious and fall within the general description of the operation of the Public Service Staff Relations Act, in the preceding section of this chapter.

The Post Office Department

The Canadian post office is at present a department of government similar to, say, the Department of Agriculture or the Department of Trade and Commerce. Like other departments in a parliamentary system, it is the responsibility of a member of the cabinet—the postmaster general—who is an elected member of Parliament. Ranking below the postmaster general is the deputy postmaster general, who is the senior civil servant and chief executive officer in the department. Headquarters in Ottawa is organized into some fifteen major branches, five of which are in the personnel area, under the immediate authority of the assistant deputy postmaster general-personnel. In the field the country is divided into fourteen districts, each headed by a district director who reports directly to the deputy postmaster general. In addition the five largest urban post offices in the country[103] have each been designated as district post offices, and the postmaster of each also reports directly to the deputy postmaster general. In fiscal year 1967-68 the post office served 4.9 million businesses and households, had 10,838 post offices in operation, and a total personnel strength of 48,376.[104]

In 1968 the new postmaster general, Eric Kierans, announced that a task force had been appointed to study the possible conversion of the post office into a public (crown) corporation.[105] Following similar developments in other countries, this change is likely to take place during the mid-1970s.

The proposal had been mooted for several years by various groups for quite different reasons. Initially the labor unions had supported the proposal to convert the post office into a crown corporation because they hoped to bring postal employees within the ambit of the private sector labor relations statute, the Industrial Relations and Disputes Investigation Act.[106] Elements in the post office management, particularly Postmaster General Kierans, supported the proposal because they believed that a crown corporation would give them the flexibility needed to bypass governmental red tape and radically to improve both service and efficiency. This hope reflects a mood parallel to that of the employee organizations, that the post office is different from the rest of the public service. Operations-oriented, post office management resents having to turn to other departments for authorization to construct new buildings or to modernize working arrangements. In 1966 the Montpetit Report[107] had recommended that a thorough study be made of the proposal to convert the post office into a crown corporation, while in 1962 the Glassco Commission[108] had also recommended changes that would allow the post office to "operate in substantially the same manner, with similar financial practices, as a utility in the private sector."[109]

Controversy over the relationship of the post office to the government centers on the issue of whether or to what extent the post office should charge its users for the full cost of its services (including in its costs an adequate wage for its employees), as against the present system of public subsidization. Generally, though not exclusively, those who feel the postal service should pay its own way also favor turning the post office into a crown corporation.

At present the management finds the existing structure extremely cumbersome. For example, the introduction of semi-autonomus servicewide or "horizontal" bargaining units makes it difficult to coordinate and impose distinctive post office personnel policies. Senior officials in the post office tend to favor a more streamlined structure which, they feel, could best be accomplished within a crown corporation. The attitude of the unions, of course, proceeds from somewhat different premises. Whether they will continue to press for this change will depend upon their experiences under the 1967 Public Service Staff Relations Act.

The 1965 Strike

Prior to the post office strike of 1965, the department had been largely ignored both by Parliament and by the public. To be sure, the signs of impending strife were there to be read after the fact. In the three or four years immediately prior to the strike, the government was attacked occasionally by an opposition member for "the revolting working conditions within the post office."[110] These attacks were almost invariably prefaced by fulsome tributes to the heroic stoicism of the post office employees and generally sloughed off as mere "opposition tactics." Yet as 1965 drew nearer it became increasingly clear both that the post office employees did have genuine grievances and that these were being ignored. Periodically newspaper stories speculated upon a crisis in the post office; questions would be raised in Parliament, brushed aside, and then forgotten. But by the spring of 1965 the situation could no longer be ignored. Both in the press and in Parliament it was charged that postal employees were getting "ridiculously low salaries," that letter carriers were "grossly underpaid,"[111] that morale in the post office was low, and that employees were leaving for other jobs. This gradual accumulation of evidence of what the prestigious Toronto *Globe and Mail* termed "miserably low" salaries, juxtaposed with a public conviction that the function of the post office was vital and required efficient, honest, and competent employees, earned the postman considerable public sympathy. In an opinion which seems representative, the *Globe and Mail* editorialized: "The vital nature [of the postal employees'] task and the responsibility with which they discharge it has earned them the admiration and respect of the great mass of Canadians. . . . [T]here is evidence of substantial public sympathy for the postmen."[112]

While occasional comments on the postman's plight were directed toward his lack of collective bargaining and arbitration rights, or toward his poor working conditions, the primary focus of the public's concern was the low level of post office salaries. The salary ranges which were effective from

October 1, 1962, until the spring of 1965 were clearly inadequate to support a household: for letter carriers the range was $3630-$4380 per year; for postal clerks grades 1 and 2 the combined salary range was $3330-$4680.[113] Approximately 55 percent of the 15,527 employees in these three groups had reached their maximum rate of pay and thus could only gain increases by a general upward adjustment of the scale.[114] The highest salary of the 22,000 operational employees of the post office was $5280 per year in 1965. Other issues—the lack of adequate labor relations mechanisms for determining salaries, and the working conditions within the post office— surfaced during the strike and received great prominence after it. But in the spring of 1965 the salary question was the one before the public.

The immediate cause of the strike also was the salary question. The Civil Service Commission had recommended in June 1965 that postal salaries be increased by $300 to $360 per year over the level set almost three years before. The Treasury Board considered this recommendation and in turn recommended it to cabinet. Only in the final stages did the minister of finance consult directly with the Postal Workers' Brotherhood, although the process of decision-making lasted from mid-June to mid-July. During that month employees of the post office in several of the larger centers decided to strike if the government approved the commission's figure of $300 to $360 rather than the $660 which they sought. When the unions' position was rejected, mass meetings were called and strike votes organized. Finally, on July 23 federal government employees struck for the first time in over forty years. It must be underlined, moreover, that this strike was not sanctioned by any extant legislation; indeed, it followed by only a few weeks the report of the Heeney Committee which envisaged a collective bargaining system without recourse to strikes.

Nor were the post office employees acting only in defiance of existing and projected public policies. They were in conflict with the directives of the national officers of the two unions and of the Postal Workers' Brotherhood. For example, in

Toronto the president of the letter carriers' union was shouted down at the meeting during which the strike vote was taken when he stated that the walkout would be illegal from the union's point of view. In fact in 1963 the national convention of the LCUC had explicitly voted against strike action. Repeatedly the brotherhood urged striking employees to return to work, but to no avail. The impetus for the strike came from the more militant local organizations, especially in the larger centers of Toronto, Montreal, Vancouver, and Windsor, a highly unionized community. As the days progressed and the effectiveness of the strike became apparent, an even wider rift developed between the postal workers and their national executive. Ultimately, the strike was directed against the relatively conservative union leadership as well as the post office management. Those who occupy positions of responsibility in the postal unions today won office in the palace revolutions following the strike: this fact must be an important determinant of their own relationships to their constituents and to government in bargaining, down to the present time.

At least in Toronto, Vancouver, and Montreal the strikers seemed well organized. Since 1958 leaders in these cities, particularly Bill Kay (letter carriers) in Vancouver and William Houle (postal workers) and Roger Decarie (letter carriers) in Montreal, had been making a conscious effort to build a "union atmosphere" among their fellow workers. Selected union members had been sent to seminars and courses conducted by the Canadian Labour Congress; they were trained in methods of organizing workers, conducting meetings, and waging economic warfare. Their training bore fruit and the strike was totally effective in the larger centers. It can fairly be said that the strike was organized—and, as will be seen, won—by local leaders, although the union today officially describes it as "spontaneous." In any event, effective industrial unionism in the post office was the most important legacy of the strike. If unionism had been espoused only by the devout few prior to 1965, thereafter it was a respectable and widely accepted creed.

The 1965 strike, as has been noted, was the first major

strike of government departmental employees in a generation. Perhaps this fact helps to explain the government's confused and somewhat desperate reactions. On the eve of the strike the government appointed Judge J. C. Anderson as a commissioner to inquire whether the salary increases which the government had already decided to grant were fair and reasonable. Next, a three-member cabinet committee was appointed to oversee the postal service "problem," and the government announced that it would not hire strikebreakers. However, it refused to state whether it would dismiss the strikers, as it apparently had authority to do under the Civil Service Act, if they were absent from work for seven days.[115]

The brotherhood's repeated pleas to the workers to return to their jobs pending the outcome of Judge Anderson's report was greeted with derision. Mr. Houle, the leader of the Montreal workers, said: "There is no question of negotiations now because there has never been any real negotiations between postal workers and Government. In the past negotiations were a sham, always immaterial, in which the Government ruled according to their own interpretation of laws and regulations. We had no say in anything, and we finally saw that this was the only way to have a say in what happens to us."[116]

As the strike stretched on, the call for a return to work was supported by some of the press. For example, the *Globe and Mail* warned the postal employees against "overplaying their hand" and suggested that a return to work at this stage would not be capitulation but "strategic withdrawal." However, the postal workers had at last begun to "have a say" and were in no mood to cease asserting themselves. In the face of this firm rank-and-file attitude, the brotherhood's executive was compelled to act and appointed a committee to meet with Judge Anderson. Although Anderson urged a return to work while his inquiry was in progress, the strikers refused to agree. No doubt their already considerable suspicion of the government was intensified by its refusal to make a public commitment to treat the commissioner's recommendations as binding. Revenue Minister Benson, on behalf of the special cabinet committee, would state only that the government would "act promptly" on the report. In addition, newspaper reports emanating from unidentified cabinet ministers made it "clear" that if the strike was not halted, the government would have no alternative but to recall Parliament and legislate an end to the walkout.[117]

The first significant breakthrough in the strike came after five days, on July 28, when Judge Anderson recommended an immediate interim pay increase of $60, in advance of his final report, which he promised would be completed within fourteen days. This recommendation resolved in favor of the union an important issue of principle, i.e. that pay increases should be granted "across the board." The $60 raise would affect the largest group of employees, who had been offered $300, and bring their increases into line with the $360 originally offered the minority. Second, Judge Anderson publicly undertook to recommend "a further substantial across the board increase" for all 23,000 employees. The prime minister stated that these recommendations "made sense" but refused to commit the government to implement them until the full report was received.

At this point the national strike scene became confused, and the unity of the strikers began to dissolve. In many centers postal employees returned to work; in others they remained on strike. On August 4 Judge Anderson recommended that the postal workers be given increases ranging in total from $510 to $550. This increase the government accepted with alacrity, the unions with reluctance. The national officers of the brotherhood urged the members to accept the offer "in spite of its limitations." William Houle, the postal workers' leader in Montreal, voted against acceptance of the report's salary rates, but his local counterpart, Roger Decarie of the letter carriers, urged his members to end the stoppage, stating that "we've squeezed just about all the juice out of the lemon."[118] Most of the post office employees agreed; the strike ended after seventeen days, on August 10. By any standard of measurement, the strike was a clear victory for the unions: it produced a significant salary increase, a sympathetic public awareness of post office working conditions, and no reprisals by the government.

The ramifications of the strike were not confined to the post office. It demonstrated to all public employers that even if the right to engage in concerted activity is not formally guaranteed—or even contemplated—by law, employees who are sufficiently frustrated, and who lack other effective means of redress, will use labor's most powerful weapon. The intense and ubiquitous discontent within the post office and the cohesion of the employees in the major centers certainly made the strike possible. That it succeeded despite the opposition of the union leadership is some measure of the depth of their feelings. Even if the government had been decisive rather than vacillatory in its actions, it probably could not have done much to induce the strikers to return to work without crossing the boundary of coercive measures unacceptable to the public at large. The post office walkout of 1965 hints that at least where a particular amalgam of circumstances exists a government functioning within the Canadian political culture is relatively powerless to prevent its employees from withdrawing their labor.

Thus the most far-reaching effect of the strike was its impact upon the developing collective bargaining relationship of government to its employees. According to the *Globe and Mail*, "the best thing to come out of the strike is the indication of Government intention to work on the introduction of collective bargaining procedures for its employees."[119] After the postal strike the Canadian conception of public service collective bargaining was fundamentally altered: the right to strike was accepted, a step which neither the Heeney Report nor most major Western governments had been prepared to take. Second, the postal employees had insisted upon bargaining with the government rather than being the mere recipients of its favors. This determination to be an equal bargaining party was reflected in the new statute. Third, the postal unions had insisted that the government be bound by Judge Anderson's report. While this demand was not accepted at the time, the new statute did bring into operation provisions which would bind the government in negotiations and arbitration proceedings. Of course, the action of the postal workers was not solely responsible for these three results. Nevertheless, it did make dramatically apparent the dissatisfaction of at least one major group of government employees, articulated their objectives in the industrial relations field, and awakened the specter of similar action on the part of other government employees.

However, at least in the short run, the strike appeared to have made even more pronounced the rift between the postal workers and their new radical leadership on the one side, and the balance of the civil service on the other. Perhaps fearful of a general public reaction against any proposed liberalization of the collective bargaining system, Claude Edwards, president of the 80,000-member Civil Service Federation, openly condemned the postal workers' actions and stated that strikes by public servants could do more harm than good. Though the CUPW had broken away from the Civil Service Federation in 1961, the LCUC had not done so. However, in 1966, following the strike, this step was taken, and both groups are now affiliated with the Canadian Labour Congress. Nonetheless, the 1965 strike did ultimately tend to radicalize the more traditional public service employee organizations. If they have not yet reestablished organizational links with the postal employees some five years later, there is now at least a greater affinity of philosophy and style, a more sympathetic attitude toward their estranged colleagues.

With regard to the post office itself, the strike brought into dramatic focus the working conditions within the department. The strike forced the government to initiate a full-scale inquiry by Mr. Justice Montpetit of the Quebec Superior Court "into the Post Office Department concerning grievances relating to work rules, codes of discipline and other conditions of employment applying to non-supervisory operating employees, exclusive of salaries."[120]

The Montpetit Report

The Inquiry Commission into working conditions in the post office, headed by Mr. Justice Montpetit, took approximately one year to receive, digest, and consider the submissions presented to it and to publish its report. The report was unique, for it was the product of the first inquiry ever conducted by the federal government at the request of employees into a specific department. In brief, its conclusion was a wide-ranging and damning indictment of working conditions in the post office. The central industrial relations problem in the post office was characterized simply as one of "human relations," and the department was censured for maintaining a working atmosphere more paramilitary than industrial.

The commission received lengthy briefs from both the CUPW and the LCUC. In their brief the postal workers said that it was essential that they be given full bargaining rights, including the right to strike, and that they be made subject to the procedures of the Industrial Relations and Disputes Investigation Act. Personnel and equipment policies were termed archaic; supervisors were classified as "inept and confused." The department was attacked on all fronts: for its practice of spying on its employees,[121] for an outmoded system of rating the efficiency of the workers, for buildings described as "badly ventilated, badly heated, very often windowless, old structures." The union also sought elimination of all-but-necessary weekend work, greater overtime pay, and two daily 15-minute coffee breaks. The brief called for a complete overhaul of the postal code of discipline and the abolition of all monetary penalties. Finally, the union attributed much of its failure to obtain the redress of grievances in the civil service in the past to the fact that most civil servants were organized in loosely knit associations which could only be described as "company unions." The letter carriers reiterated many of the postal workers' submissions, particularly in regard to the demand for full industrial bargaining rights, the severe attacks on the unsanitary working conditions prevailing within the post offices, and the complaints voiced about the heavy disciplinary penalties meted out to employees. Also advocated by the letter carriers were twice-daily mail deliveries, an end to all mail addressed "To the Householder," a 35-hour week, and a complete revamping of the system of overtime pay.

In general terms[122] the report upheld most of the employees' grievances, stating that "except in one or two districts . . . supervisors and postmasters . . . have only a vague notion of the importance of maintaining good relations with their staff." The report condemned the management for too often considering itself "almost infallible." "Under the pretext of maintaining at any cost their conception of order and discipline," the report continued, the management "obstinately refuse to change any decisions taken at a lower level."[123]

Most essential, in the view of the report, was the development of a "well-conceived policy of consultation and of exchange of viewpoints at all levels." With the advent of collective bargaining, the necessity for communication between employees and employers with good faith on both sides would become even more essential. The employees' representatives were admonished that they too would have to become "more conciliatory, more understanding, and more reasonable."

The report contained 282 recommendations, many of a detailed and technical nature. Several topics deserve to be highlighted here. On collective bargaining[124] the report made two recommendations. First, it rejected the employees' submission that the post office be turned into a crown corporation and that it be placed under the private sector labor relations statute, instead suggesting a study be made of the advisability of according the post office this status. This study now seems likely to produce affirmative results, with the consequence that postal employees may ultimately be freed from the unwilling embrace of the Public Service Staff Relations Act. Second, it recommended that the employees give a "fair trial" to the collective bargaining procedures under the new Public Service Staff Relations Act. Next, the report recommended that joint employer-employee councils be set up on a local basis and at the national level to process grievances dealing with working conditions; that a grievance procedure be implemented, and that the employees have recourse to binding adjudication. Finally, on working conditions, the report made a comprehensive series of recommendations which were directed toward civilizing the work pattern of postal employees as far as possible.

The Montpetit Report received wide publicity when it was published in October 1966, and editorial comment was virtually unanimous in castigating the post office for what the *Globe and Mail* called its "moss-back atmosphere."[125] Its findings not only influenced salary negotiations over the next several years, but by November 1968 some 200 of its recommendations had been implemented in whole or in part;[126] many of the remainder are still under negotiation between the Council of Postal Unions and the government. While the impact of the Commission on the Post Office was thus indisputable, its influence was more pervasive yet. For the first time industrial relations within a government department were systematically subjected to comparison with those in the private sector and found completely wanting. The report therefore may be considered an important step in the transition of the public sector to full collective bargaining, in the sense that it helped to dispel the myth of benevolence which had surrounded the traditional public employment system.

The Joint Committee Hearings

The militancy exhibited during the 1965 strike did not abate when the employees returned to work. It merely shifted from the picket lines to the parliamentary committee rooms.

In 1966 the special joint committee of the Senate and the House of Commons[127] conducted hearings and heard evidence submitted by interested parties on the proposed Public Service Staff Relations Act and associated legislation. Both postal unions presented briefs to the committee, and officers of both unions were questioned by its members.[128] While the unions welcomed the advent of collective bargaining for government employees, they had deep reservations about the wisdom of applying the provisions of the proposed legislation to the post office. It is proposed here merely to outline these reservations. (The submissions of both unions covered virtually identical points and did not contradict each other in any material way.)

The essence of their submissions is contained in Mr. Decarie's statement that, "It is not a question of being under any type of bill at all; we want one under which we can negotiate freely everything that concerns us as employees, just as any other citizen in the country."[129] Hence any features of the new bill which appeared to infringe upon this objective were bitterly attacked as being restrictive and unwarranted.

The postal employees looked upon themselves as fulfilling a quasi-commercial function which in their view made the post office more closely analogous to a crown corporation than to any other department of government. This position led them to reject the Montpetit Report's recommendation that they try out the new act, and to insist that they be brought under the Industrial Relations and Disputes Investigation Act. Since crown corporations are regulated in their industrial relations by the IRDI Act, the postal unions concluded that the post office would also have to be made a crown corporation. They pointed to the long history and voluminous body of precedent developed under the IRDI Act, stated that the new act was more restrictive, and expressed preference over the new untried and complicated legislation for a statute which they knew worked well. In the words of the CUPW brief, it was "like throwing away a perfectly good outboard motor and substituting paddles."

As well as these general complaints, the postal employees had a number of specific concerns arising out of novel provisions of the Public Service Staff Relations Act. Since both unions were "unalterably opposed to compulsory arbitration in any form," and since they assumed (correctly) that most other public service employee organizations would eschew the conciliation-strike alternative in favor of compulsory arbitration, the letter carriers claimed the new act aided and abetted "company unionism." Their fear of employer domination was also manifest in their attack upon the procedure for appointing the Public Service Staff Relations Board (PSSRB) and its adjunct agencies. The CUPW was unable to distinguish between the government as employer and its executive and legislative roles, and was "uncomfortable" in the knowledge that the PSSRB would be selected and appointed by the employer and thus presumptively beholden to it for tenure, remuneration, and reappointment. In fact, the unions charged, because the IRDI Act did not contain enough "employer control devices," a new statute had been devised "in order to make certain that federal public employees would not fall under the influence of the legitimate trade union movement of the country."

In their comments about the restrictive nature of the new statute, the postal employees concentrated upon three points. First, they charged that most of the conditions of employment and methods of discipline would be outside the scope of collective bargaining. In the words of the LCUC brief, "The Government strikes us as an expert poker player who has himself shuffled the cards and dealt himself all the aces. It cannot lose." The sections of the act (discussed above) which prohibit the Arbitration Tribunal and conciliation boards from dealing with the "standards, procedures or processes governing the appointment, appraisal, promotion, demotion, transfer, layoff or release of employees" were roundly castigated. The postal employees urged that these matters be left open to collctive bargaining and that suitable terms be devised by negotiation. Second, the unions argued that the statutory language giving the employer the final authority "to determine the organization of the Public Service and to assign duties and classify positions therein" was inequitable. Instead, it was argued, these matters should also have been made negotiable. Third, a prohibition against the PSSRB certifying any employee organization which contributes financially to any political party was attacked as an "outright prohibition of political activities on the part of public employees."

In short, the testimony of the postal unions displayed an outspoken preference for private sector legislation. Where the new statute departed from the private sector model in any significant degree, it was treated with suspicion and hostility.

However, the postal workers did not prevail. The new statute did come into force and did cover the post office department. To what extent have the fears of the postal unions proved to be well founded? To what extent have the postal unions been able to secure their interests under it?

Bargaining Under the Public Service Staff Relations Act

The new statutory regime began somewhat inauspiciously for the postal unions. Rebuffed, as has been recounted above, in their first attempt to gain bargaining rights, they early experienced frustrations in the processing of grievances and in other attempts to check unilateral employer action. In part these failures and frustrations were the result of a lack of expertise within the ranks of the unions' staff and officials; in part they were a result of limitations inherent in the statutory scheme.

However, the ultimate test of the new legislation, for the postal unions, would be the facility with which a new and acceptable collective agreement could be negotiated. The process proved to be long and difficult, and the outcome of negotiations less than satisfactory. The new statute came into force in March 1967, but an agreement was not negotiated for almost eighteen months. As will be seen, its terms were far from the unions' objectives.

The postal employees had begun their last prestatutory pay discussions in 1966 flushed with the success of 1965, and they pressed for an hourly pay increase of $1.00. In the summer of 1966 the government had settled a strike of St. Lawrence Seaway workers by granting a well-publicized 30 percent wage increase, and the postal workers had this and several other precedents before them. Aside from the wage issue, the postal employees were concerned with the government's unilateral action in reclassifying positions within the post office, as part of a general program of classification revision recommended by the Civil Service Commission. They claimed not only that the reclassification scheme should have been delayed until the advent of collective bargaining, but that it was working to the particular disadvantage of those who had participated in the 1965 strike.

Early in the 1966 negotiations, authorization to call a strike was received by the union leaders, and armed with this mandate they rejected the wage increases offered by the Civil Service Commission. In the end a strike was averted and the postal employees accepted a modest $.25 per-hour wage increase and a ten-month contract. However, little was really settled; the conflict was merely postponed temporarily. The Ottawa *Citizen* editorialized:

It must be remembered that somewhere at the roots of this labor dispute is the anger generated by the injustices and grossly archaic working conditions tabulated by Mr. Justice Montpetit in his 350 page report. True the workers today are talking solely about salaries, but the mood encountered by Mr. Justice Montpetit, which he described as their alarming unwillingness to compromise, pervades the present discussions. It must be cured at its source.[130]

In order to get to the "source," a joint union-management committee was set up in November 1966 to find ways and means of expeditiously implementing the Montpetit Report recommendations. The Council of Postal Unions had been generally unhappy with the pace and manner of implementation. It claimed that only minor recommendations had received the attention of the post office and that recommendations were deemed to be "implemented" once they were agreed to. On the other hand, the unions considered recommendations implemented only when they had been fully carried out in every post office.[131]

By the time that the next round of salary negotiations began in 1967-68 (the first under the new statute), the "poor human relations" which Judge Montpetit had singled out as the most troublesome aspect of employment in the post office had certainly not been eradicated. The climate was hardly conducive to effective collective bargaining.

The first three months of negotiations ended in late April 1968 with both sides reporting frustration; in the postal unions' view, the three months had passed "without worthwhile progress." The president of the CUPW stated: "While I do not accuse the Treasury Board representatives of bargaining in bad faith, I did draw a personal conclusion that they were either incapable of bargaining and reaching an agreement or were stalling so that a third party could resolve the dispute through the conciliation process."[132]

Pursuant to the provisions of the act, the CPU applied for the appointment of a conciliation board when the talks were broken off, a condition precedent to the right to strike. While the composition of the board was being determined,

Judge Rene Lippe of the Quebec Provincial Court was named as informal, nonstatutory mediator. His efforts were unsuccessful, and a conciliation board was appointed in due course under the chairmanship of Professor Andre Desgagne of Laval University. The report of the board records its success in resolving many differences relating to working conditions, but it was unable to reach the issue of wages within the time available to it. Again following the provisions of the act, a strike date was set, and the first strike under the government's new staff relations legislation began on schedule on July 18.

Until literally the day before the strike was due to begin, the government made no wage offer. Early in the negotiations the CPU had demanded a $.75 increase over a 14-month contract period for all but two categories of workers (for whom they demanded a $.95 per hour increase). Then on July 17 the government finally offered a $.15 increase for a one-year contract. Predictably this offer was greeted by the unions' William Houle as a "big joke." The government's second offer came on July 31 only after a further two weeks of intensive mediation by Judge Lippe, who had resumed his vital though unofficial efforts: a $.49 increase to be awarded in three stages stretched out over a 38-month period. The final settlement came a week later—a $.39 raise to be paid out over a 26-month contract. This wage increase represented a gain of approximately 15 percent. Far below the raise originally agitated for by the unions, it was not significantly above the initial government offer. Nonetheless, after almost three weeks of striking, the postal employees narrowly agreed to capitulate. What produced this unexpected decline in their fortunes?

At the outset of the strike, public opinion had favored the postal workers. The Toronto *Telegram* noted that the maximum wage paid in the leading categories of postal workers was $5735 per year and asked "Who can live on that amount in Canada today?"[133] However, as the strike progressed, editorials began to call for a reassessment of the legislation which gave government employees a right to strike.[134] Yet throughout the strike the government refused to retreat from the new statutory scheme, although the prime minister vaguely threatened that his government would have "to look at further means if the discussions were to go on endlessly and the parties were to appear to be worlds apart." Mr. Trudeau set two conditions for summoning Parliament to deal with the strike: first, that the right to strike extended to civil servants under the PSSR Act was being used with clear irresponsibility; and second, that the hardships on the country were so great that the public would wish to reverse its recent decision and take away the strike right.[135] In the opinion of the government, neither of these events occurred, and the strike was allowed to run its course. While the threat of government intervention did hang rather vaguely over the negotiators, it was never seriously considered a possibility by the union leaders. The technical operations of the post office required a trained staff which could not easily be replaced by other personnel, and measures necessary to coerce the postal employees to return to their jobs would have required legislative changes in the new act. Moreover, the success of such changes, especially if introduced as a "strike-breaking" measure, was wholly uncertain.

It can fairly be said, then, that the determination of the government to play out its role as a tough collective bargaining adversary was a major factor in the outcome of the strike. Despite some public criticism of the alleged inexperience and ineptitude of the government (and union) negotiators, it is clear that the uncertainty and confusion of 1965 had been substantially dispelled by 1968.

In part, too, the government simply had to hold firm as a political matter. Its self-imposed antiinflationary wage guideline of approximately 6 percent annually had attracted favorable publicity. In the Toronto *Star's* words, "To abandon it would be to abandon the government's fight against inflation through exemplary wage restraint. And Canada cannot afford that."[136] In the press little attention was paid to the absolute increases demanded by the workers; in an inflationary period there was more concern with the percentage increases sought. The Treasury Board admitted that the postal workers lagged behind in dollar terms, but stated that the reason for this was that the postal employees were unskilled in comparison with other public and private sector groups.

To be sure, government was able to hold the line in 1968 because the experience of 1965 had shown that the mail service was not, in fact, an indispensable amenity or a virtual economic necessity. Despite some inconvenience and extra cost, both individual citizens and businesses were able to survive reasonably well by making alternative arrangements for the duration of the strike. Whether, and how, a longer strike might have changed the public pressure on the government is not known. However, at least initially there seemed to be little political risk attached to waging the conflict as a private employer would.

Although union morale was initially high, it can hardly be said that the CPU was totally prepared for the strike. Its leadership was by no means secure in office. Having come to power as a result of a membership revolt in 1965, they were very much aware of the risks of any apparent willingness to compromise with the government. Moreover, in retrospect the union leadership is convinced that they were too closely bound by mandates given to them at their national conventions, and they have since reorganized their procedure to give the negotiating team more flexibility. In addition to insecure leadership, the unions also obviously suffered from lack of a fund to pay strike pay. Finally, perhaps reflecting the first two points, the union's initial bargaining objective of $.75 per hour was simply not realistic, given the political and economic position of the government and the lack of resources within the union to conduct a sustained strike effort.

Naturally, this kind of rational analysis would hardly recommend itself to most strikers. Although the workers finally voted to accept the government's offer, the settlement was not greeted very enthusiastically. In Vancouver and Montreal it was rejected and in Toronto approved by a bare 50.5 percent. In effect the smaller centers carried the vote in favor of settlement. It was widely recognized that the final offers did not approach the original demands although the *Postal Tribune* found what satisfaction it could "in a wide range of improvements in working conditions, including better arrangements for grievances, seniority and overtime pay."[137]

Thus while the unions did lose the strike in terms of wage gains, they are convinced that some benefits did accrue to them. They fully utilized their rights under the act and demonstrated their determination not to be cowed; their baptism of fire thrust them into even closer affinity with the industrial unions. Their real "victory," if any, seems to have come in the area of greater solidarity and organizational sophistication. To some extent its manifestations can be seen in the tight discipline and tactical adroitness of the CPU in the 1970 negotiations (still in progress at the date of writing).

"Human Relations" and Contract Administration
Under the Public Service Staff Relations Act

There is little doubt that the basic problem described by Mr. Justice Montpetit has not been solved to any appreciable extent. Some of the reasons for the continuing hostility between employer and employee directly affect the stance taken by the parties in collective bargaining. One factor is the type of function carried out by the department. The traditional post office attitude holds that the "mail must go through" whenever it arrives, and "damn the employees." Since mail arrives in post offices at odd hours, and since the tradition is still operative, working conditions are unusual and in themselves create tension. While the unions conjure up analogies to industry, the fact remains that as long as the post office and its employees remain oriented toward a traditional operations stance, the conditions of work in the post office will be different from those prevailing in industry. The unions' search for conditions of work similar to those enjoyed by the semiskilled industrial worker collides with management's commitment to old traditions of service. Perhaps these clashes can be softened only by regular shifts with their resulting impact on mail distribution.

A second factor inhibiting the development of good staff relations is the uneasy alliance between the two major unions and, especially in the LCUC, the tenuous grasp of union officers on the reins of power. Postal administrators find it difficult to deal with the unions not only because of the antagonism existing between management and the employees, but because they cannot be sure that an understanding once reached can be executed by the union leadership. There is some indication that a better working relationship is growing between postal administrators and the CUPW, as the leadership of that union has begun to consolidate diverse factions and to impose its will with more authority.

A third factor aggravating good relations is the attitude of management toward the union and its general ineptness in personnel matters. While there are many management deficiencies, however, it should be reemphasized that management should not be forced to assume the entire mantle of blame.

At the level of first-line supervisors, friction exists between the employees and management. Recruited from a base which is not particularly able, often appointed on the basis of internal patronage, and paid at a level which is not significantly higher than those immediately under them, these supervisors are little respected and tend to be threatened by the union as a competing source of authority. At higher levels the post office management has not completely accepted the fact of unionism. Failure to accept the union often stems not so much from antipathy toward it but rather from a lack of understanding of the pervasive cooperation needed between management and labor. Moreover, the structure of the post office in the past has abetted the development of autonomous local administrators, in part because long years of neglect left the department virtually without an effective central administration. At best it is a long and laborious process for central personnel management to impress upon field management the type of atmosphere which is essential to good industrial relations. The process is particularly difficult when the two represent opposing traditions within the postal service. Very recently, with the advent of a new and determined minister, the post office has been infused with management personnel from other government departments and from private industry.

On the whole the relations of these new arrivals with the unions are better, but the operations sector, staffed by men recruited from the ranks, remains indifferent, if not hostile.

Even at the highest level, naivete persists concerning the need to initiate full and meaningful discussions with labor. The 1969 decision to implement five-day mail distribution and to alter the method of delivery was taken without consulting either the union or the post office's own personnel directors, despite the profound personnel implications of these operational changes. The CPU filed a grievance claiming that the collective agreement had been violated in that working conditions had been altered without prior consultation. In his decision,[138] sustaining the grievance, the chief adjudicator scathingly denounced post office attitudes as arrogant and high-handed. His decision continued:

> Hostility, vindictiveness, and possibly distrust appear to frustrate any opportunity for effective inter-relationships. It would appear that the senior officials in the Post Office Department have not as yet reconciled themselves to operating the postal facilities within a progressive collective bargaining atmosphere. . . . The Employer by its conduct was primarily responsible for frustrating the opportunity for consultation by crystallizing management decisions prior to dealing with the Bargaining Agent representatives.[139]

Two other adjudications[140] published at the same time made comments in a similar vein, and the new delivery procedure was finally abandoned. Sheer inability to understand completely and fully the necessity for working in tandem with the employee organizations is the major problem confounding post office staff relations. Failure to work with the unions is not necessarily founded on conscious malice, nor is this attitude confined to the post office. But it is perhaps most painfully obvious in the post office, of all federal government departments, that much remains to be done if the principles and institutions rooted in the legislation are to bring about genuine labor-management harmony and decent working conditions.

·IV·

The Formal Public Sector Model: Collective Bargaining by Police Forces in Ontario

THE collective bargaining system of police in Ontario is highly structured, although distinctly different from a private sector system. Police work is concerned with the protection of persons, property, and public order.[1] It is therefore not surprising to find that police employment disputes are to be settled by arbitration without stoppage of work, and that employer-employee relationships are authoritarian and paramilitary rather than bilateral and democratic. What is perhaps surprising is the degree to which these distinctive characteristics of police personnel policies are rapidly being brought into question.

The Organization and Structure of Police Forces in Ontario

Excluding the federal Royal Canadian Mounted Police, there are two types of police forces in Ontario: the Ontario Provincial Police (OPP) and the municipal police forces. The municipal police forces have jurisdiction within organized municipalities, while the OPP serve sparsely populated areas, which do not have their own forces.

In relation to their police functions, both the OPP and the municipal forces are regulated by the Police Act[2] and regulations made under it. Collective bargaining and arbitration procedures for municipal police are also established by this statute, while the Public Service Act[3] which governs the provincial government's employees also applies to the OPP. This analysis will deal with the municipal police forces, since the collective bargaining system under the Public Service Act is described elsewhere.

The obligation of a municipality to provide police services may be discharged in one of several ways: if its population is more than 15,000 the municipal council will appoint a board of commissioners of police which must then appoint the police; if its population is less than 15,000 a police commission is either optional or may only be appointed with the consent of the attorney-general, according to the size of the population. If no police commission is appointed, the town council must appoint the police directly, although under certain circumstances the Police Act allows a municipality to conclude an agreement with either the OPP or with another municipality under which police services will be provided.

While it is clear that there is a statutory obligation placed upon the municipality to satisfy the need for police services within the municipality, the members of the police force are not "employees" or "servants" of the municipality in the ordinary sense of these terms.[4] Their duties are of a public nature and defined by statute rather than by the command of their employer. Thus a court has stated that a police constable is a "ministerial officer exercising statutory rights independently of contract."[5] These rights and duties are the subject of regulations made under the Police Act which apply to members of all police forces in the province, although municipalities may make additional regulations "not inconsistent" with the provincial directives.

However, this position is more theoretical than real. The police commission or council, as the case may be, in fact acts as the police employer in the municipality. It bargains collectively with its "employees"; it may contract, sue, and be sued; and it has the power to summon and examine witnesses under oath. Where a commission is appointed, it generally consists of the head of the municipal council, a county or district court judge, and "one other person."[6] The latter two members are appointed by the provincial government, which retains real control over the appointments, often using the third seat as a reward for political endeavors. Most often the judge is the dominant figure on the board. He is professionally concerned with the administration of criminal justice, possesses significant social prestige, and enjoys an appointment (unlike his colleagues) which carries no limit of time. Especially in a smaller community his influence is paramount. Moreover, some judges sit on several police commissions simultaneously, and at least one Ontario judge sits on no less than five. These factors combine to produce a commission immune from public pressures, an aid no doubt to honest police administration but apt to generate authoritarian administrative attitudes that are inimical to collective bargaining. The present structure of police commissions is under attack by civil liberties groups and others concerned with citizen-police relations. No doubt reforms generated as a result of these other concerns will help to ease collective bargaining relationships.[7]

Assuming, however, that the police commission device continues to be employed as the principal instrument for administering the affairs of the force, its relationship to the municipal council must be examined. The municipal council, of course, has a primary obligation to provide police services, but it discharges this obligation through the commission. However, the council retains the power to tax and to spend. How is financial responsibility squared with the responsibility to provide service?

The commission is given power to determine the adequacy of the force and its equipment and is required to submit its annual budget estimates to the council. In the event of disagreement between the two bodies on either the adequacy of the force or the estimates, the dispute is to be determined by the provincially appointed Ontario Police Commission, described below.[8] Moreover, as will be seen, the commission has power to negotiate binding collective agreements with its employees or, failing agreement, to carry a negotiation dispute forward to binding arbitration. In either event the municipal council is required to meet the financial burden thus incurred as of the beginning of the next fiscal period. Indeed, if timely notice to bargain is served, the council in preparing its next budget "shall make such provision as in its opinion is adequate for the payment of any expenditure resulting" from an agreement or award which becomes effective after the beginning of the next fiscal period.[9]

Thus both the policing function and the administration of the force are "depoliticized," and there is little direct intervention by the council in the negotiating process. Moreover, the balance between the cost of policing and other municipal functions is not ultimately struck by the council but by the Ontario Police Commission.

The Ontario Police Commission, consisting of three persons appointed by the provincial government, is ultimately responsible for controlling and coordinating all police forces in the province. Of course the commission reports to the legislature, the responsible minister being the attorney-general and minister of justice. This cabinet position has been under some strain because of the essential duality of its functions. On the one hand, the minister is in effect the civilian head of the police and is their representative in the government; on the other hand, he is the "province's lawyer," responsible for the proper administration of justice. These two roles may be in conflict, because on occasion the policing function may be seen to run counter to due process considerations which are the attorney-general's special concern. There is wide speculation that in the near future a second cabinet post will be created, that of solicitor-general, to superintend police operations in the province and to revitalize the police forces and the police commissions.

In addition to its general coordinating functions, the Ontario Police Commission conducts investigations into municipal police forces and hears appeals by members of the police forces in the province from adverse rulings made by boards, councils, or the commission of the OPP. A fairly stringent and elaborate code of discipline, recently amended, applies both to the provincial police and to the municipal forces. In certain circumstances an appeal lies to the OPC. Offenses categorized as "major" or "minor," and as it now stands appeals to the OPC, lie as a matter of right in the case of a major offense and are within the discretion of the OPC in the case of a minor offense. (The grievance procedure is discussed in detail below.) The provincial government has also established minimum qualifications for entrance into the municipal forces, minimum clothing issues, and minimum rates of pay for the municipal boards of commissioners of police. All of these provisions are enforced by the OPC.

The local police associations and their province-wide organization, the Police Association of Ontario, are quite unhappy with the composition and attitudes of the Ontario Police Commission. In their view, because the OPC is charged with overseeing all aspects of the police function in the province, it acts in reality as a management agency. This impression is reinforced by the fact that it is largely staffed by ex-senior officers from the province's police forces. The police associations have urged that the OPC be reconstituted and that it assume a more impartial role in its governing functions.

This controversy came to a head in 1969 when the province-wide police discipline code[10] was extensively revised and amendments to the Police Act were proposed by the OPC to the attorney-general, and actually introduced by him in the legislature. These amendments[11] (discussed more extensively below) had the overall effect of enhancing the power of the OPC vis-à-vis the police, but appear to have been unilaterally formulated by the OPC, without consultation or concurrence by police representatives. By way of example, the OPC proposals (which were ultimately abandoned) would have denied the right to counsel in discipline proceedings, other than so-called major offenses, and would have also precluded representation by PAO staff. As a result of PAO protests, the proposed legislative amendments were extensively revised by the government and the new discipline code is now under searching review.

This controversy has been described in order to demonstrate the prevailing attitudes of the OPC, a matter of increasing concern at a time when the movement to real collective bargaining is well under way in most police forces throughout the province. If the OPC is to assume arbitral or adjudicative functions under this new bilateral relationship, it must at least appear to be impartial, an appearance it does not yet enjoy.

In most municipalities the members of the police force have formed associations which bargain collectively for them. Together with the OPP Association these municipal police associations are affiliated to (and pay dues to) the Police Association of Ontario. PAO employs a staff of six officers who keep abreast of collective bargaining developments, advise the local associations, assist them in negotiations with police commissions, and represent individual members at discipline hearings. PAO also represents its constituent organizations in lobbying and public relations activities.

Virtually all police forces employ "civilian" personnel, who are also covered by the terms of the Police Act. In 1964 the Ontario High Court had held that motor mechanics employed to repair and maintain police vehicles were not members of the police force within the meaning of the Police Act and were consequently free to bargain collectively under the Labour Relations Act. The court reasoned that:

> The purpose of excepting a member of a police force from the provisions of the Labour Relations Act must be that such officer or constable shall always be free to fulfil his duties in the mainstream of law and order; as the only part that the employees herein play in such a responsibility, is the maintenance of the vehicles used by police officers, it would appear to be beyond the purpose of the Act to exclude them therefrom.[12]

In spite of the logic of this position, the 1964 decision was overturned by legislation.[13] Thus if civilian employees are to be represented for collective bargaining purposes, they must be represented by the association which represents uniformed officers, in which they are bound to be a small and likely ineffectual minority.

The position of civilian employees is more vulnerable yet. Membership in a local police association is not a right enjoyed by any uniformed or civilian member of the force, but is dependent upon whether the association votes him into membership. This situation has been characterized by a 1968 High Court decision[14] as "a piece of outrageous arrogance," but the discretion vested in associations has in fact enabled them to deny membership and bargaining representation to civilian employees in some centers. It seems anomalous on the one hand to deny civilian employees private sector collective bargaining rights and on the other hand to permit their exclusion from a police association which (as will be seen) enjoys a statutory monopoly to bargain with the local board of police commissioners.

THE BARGAINING REPRESENTATIVE

The Police Act provides a framework for "collective" bargaining, although it does not require the actual participation of a bargaining agent, as in the private sector.

Each police commission or council is required to bargain in good faith upon receipt of a request to do so.[15] However, this request may come either from a majority of the members of the police force or (if not less than 50 percent of the police force belong to an association) then from that association. This arrangement makes formal "certification" machinery unnecessary, because presumably any challenge to the majority status of an association can be countered by the giving of a request to bargain by the requisite number of individuals. On the other hand, no group comprising less than 50 percent of the force may submit a bargaining request, except for senior officers, who bargain separately. To date there have been no contests between rival groups claiming the right of representation. Police are prohibited from joining an association which is connected with any private sector labor organization, and under the Police Act it is an offense for any person (including a policeman) to "cause disaffection" among the members of a police force or to induce or attempt to induce a member of a police force to withhold his labor.[16]

The members of the bargaining committee on the employee side must all be members of the local police force. Over the past few years the severely limiting effect of this provision has been softened. Members of the committee may now be "accompanied" by other individuals who attend in an "advisory capacity." Where the local police association belongs to a larger police association, a member of the latter organization who is "actively engaged in the occupation of a police officer" may attend. In 1968 the police bargaining teams were allowed to be accompanied by one legal counsel and "one other advisor"; the commissions were also allowed these two additional advisors.

These rather modest concessions, coupled with the prohibition on affiliation with nonpolice labor organizations, underline the limited function envisaged by the legislation for the bargaining representatives. However, the legislative prescription is now beginning to chafe.

At the most obvious level the increasing complexity of police negotiations (reflecting trends in the private sector) now demands careful staff preparation, as well as expert representation at the bargaining table and at arbitration. Thus professionalization of association staff has been inevitable, and attempts by police commissions to prevent it have been doomed to failure. The point is vividly illustrated by the continuing harassment of the president of the Metropolitan Toronto Police Association, Sydney Brown, by the Metro Police Commission. A former active policeman, Brown has been "on leave" for some years in order to work full-time on the MTPA payroll. By first attempting to discharge him, then to compel him to return to active duty, and finally to turn in his uniform, the commission underlined precisely how effectively he was serving his constituents.

Perhaps less obvious but more serious in the long run is the process of radicalization of the police which seems to be proceeding on a continental, perhaps worldwide, basis. In brief, the police appear to feel that they have suffered a loss of prestige in the community which has not been offset by a compensatory increase in economic status. More and more North American policemen have been turning to political action as a means of coping with the economic problem. This thesis will be explored in greater detail below in a consideration of recent experience in Canada's two major cities, Toronto and Montreal.

BARGAINING AND DISPUTE RESOLUTION

The Police Act provides that a collective agreement may establish "remuneration, pensions, sick leave credit gratuities, grievance procedures or working conditions of the members of the police force . . . except such working conditions as are governed by a regulation made by the Lieutenant-Governor in Council under the Act."[17] If, following negotiations over these matters, agreement is not reached between a police association and the employer (a police commission), the dispute is to be referred to a tripartite board of arbitration, one member of which is to be nominated by each side and the third, neutral, member by the two nominees. If the third member is not agreed upon, the attorney-general makes the appointment.[18] The award of an arbitration board is binding upon municipality and police force alike, until replaced by a new agreement or award. As noted, if no agreement has been reached by the date at which the council passes its estimates for the following year, the council is required to make "adequate provision" for the payment of any expenditure resulting from a new agreement or award. This requirement makes it difficult for employer to plead "inability to pay," at least in the literal sense.

In 1969, Bill 178, An Act to Amend the Police Act, was introduced in the Ontario legislature and sparked extensive debate[19] on the role of the Ontario Police Commission, on the extent to which the elected provincial government should exercise real control over the municipal police forces, and on the procedures for negotiating and arbitrating collective agreements between the police forces and the local commissions. Since the debate aired a number of the more significant problems in municipal police labor relations, the controversy can be examined with some profit.

Bill 178, as initially drafted, was intended to accomplish four main objectives.

First, power to appoint neutral member of boards of arbitration was transferred from the attorney-general to the provincial cabinet. This change recognized the attorney-general's special, somewhat partisan role in police management and substituted a more impartial appointing agency; it was embodied in the law with little debate.

Second, Bill 178 gave to the OPC power to regulate the use of any equipment by a police force in Ontario. While important, this change is beyond our immediate purview. However, public concern was expressed because it was felt that the OPC was being given *carte blanche* to permit the use of controversial devices such as MACE and wire-tapping. The government was criticized for failing to make the OPC more directly responsive to the legislature, and it agreed under pressure to amend the bill. As amended, the OPC's regulatory power in this area is made explicitly "subject to the approval of the attorney-general," who is, of course, politically accountable. No doubt the government's retreat on this point paved the way for an about-face (as will be seen) in relation to the role of the OPC in the collective bargaining system.

Third, the bill provided that senior officers and civilians employed in a confidential or supervisory capacity might form separate bargaining units. A controversy had arisen over the resignation of 76 senior officers from the Metropolitan Toronto Police Association in 1966, following a three-year period during which they had been treated differently than the rest of the police force by the metropolitan police commission, and had not in fact been actively represented by the MTPA. Reasons given for their resignation were numerous: a belief that the senior officers were not being properly represented by the association; resentment that a "mere constable"[20] was acting as bargaining agent for senior officers and that his salary exceeded that of some senior officers, and resentment at the association's active role in representing police officers and in freely using the news media to further its ends. The bill, then, was intended to take account of this existing situation in Toronto and gave "separate but equal" bargaining and arbitration rights to senior officers and civilians employed in a confidential capacity. The attorney-general in the debate on the bill pointed out[21] that the section was optional and that because of the great number of small forces in which there were only a few senior officers, it was highly likely that in the majority of instances the section would not come into play at all. He added that the OPP system in which there was a distinction for bargaining purposes between those who held the rank above staff sergeant and those below that rank had "worked well."

This, he said, was "perhaps the strongest point" in favor of his proposal.

The amendment was attacked as a transparent attempt to fragment the bargaining unit, and its result was foreseen as bringing "senior officers in small forces under the direct influence of the local governing authority."[22] Police ranks throughout Ontario have not yet been standardized, and the OPC has sole power to determine who is a "senior officer" in the event of controversy. Thus, the police associations alleged, there is a real risk that bargaining units might be gerrymandered in order to weaken their effectiveness. The police associations further believed that withdrawal from the MTPA had in practice been a condition of promotion to senior rank, and feared that the amendment would not only encourage this practice across the remainder of the province but would also produce a clear labor-management dichotomy which would be foreign to the tradition of Ontario police forces. Opposition members in the legislature[23] saw this development as a threat to the tradition of homogeneity in the police forces and as promoting a bureaucratized paramilitary force on the American model. Withdrawal of senior officers from the bargaining unit and from the police associations might, it was feared, accelerate their existing tendency to "lord it over" their inferiors, license their interference with the traditional discretion of the individual constable, and impair their rapport with rank-and-file constables who must ultimately enforce the law.

While these fears probably have some merit, the police associations' traditional view is not entirely credible in the setting of a contemporary Canadian city. Neither British "constable" nor American "cop," the urban policeman in Canada has lost many of the traditions of the former without receiving the benefits of the latter's modern professional police administration. It seems too late to say that the senior officers are not at least to some degree "management," and the bill probably accurately reflects the need for an arm's-length relationship. It may even help to turn some senior officers into professional administrators, a development which would not be unwelcome.

The final feature of Bill 178 to be examined—most significant for this study—relates to the projected assignment to the OPC of important third party functions in the police collective bargaining system. Under the bill the OPC would be the final arbiter of grievances relating to the application or violation of collective agreements or arbitral awards made in negotiation disputes, and of controversies over the scope of collective bargaining between the parties. Following violent objections by the police and the opposition parties, these provisions were radically altered. The arbitration of differences arising between the two parties (other than discipline matters) is now to be assigned to ad hoc tripartite boards of arbitration, as in the private sector. Disputes over the proper scope of bargaining, if not resolved by the parties, are to be decided by the arbitration board constituted to decide the other substantive issues following the breakdown of negotiations.

The argument against the bill was forcefully expressed in a submission by the Police Association of Ontario to the government:

> Inasmuch as this legislation promotes the Ontario Police Commission as a final and binding referee in disputes involving bargaining, grievance procedure, arbitrations and the final and binding determination of disputes arising from these matters, we are absolutely and strongly opposed to the management oriented and management controlled Commission acting in this capacity. Experience had indicated that the Ontario Police Commission are not only influenced by management, they are in fact and in principle the *"Management Organization."*[24]

In the legislature the bill was vigorously attacked. For example, it was pointed out that since the OPC had authority to provide advice to local police commissions, under the proposed rules the OPC would be called upon to arbitrate its own advice if such advice were to be first applied by the local board and then subsequently to become the very cause of the grievance. Since it was so clearly demonstrated that the police—already denied the right to strike—would now be denied as well a fair system of arbitration, the bill was bound to undergo the significant changes listed above. In retrospect, it seems evident that the bill had been formulated by the OPC and not carefully examined by the government before it was introduced. The OPC is regarded by all the police in Ontario as "management," a view to which the whole incident lends credence. So long as the OPC retains this reputation it would be grossly unfair to accord it the powers of an independent tribunal.

While it is true to say that Ontario police associations have enjoyed the right of free collective bargaining and compulsory arbitration for twenty-five years, until relatively recently these rights were little more than statutory declarations. It was not until the emergence of strong police associations in Toronto and at the provincial level that the rights gathered real significance. In the early 1960s both groups acquired full-time presidents and expanded staffs. This development went hand in hand with an increased awareness of the advantages of collective action among nonblue-collar workers generally in Canada. Over the last decade, and more especially in the last five years, the flavor of collective bargaining between police associations and their employers has changed dramatically.

As has been noted, the legislation has steadily evolved so as to permit greater participation in local bargaining by professional police representatives and by neutral third parties. The formerly obsequious police associations now bolstered by the presence of PAO advisers who have nothing to fear from a local police commission have become self-assertive. Prior to the last few years local police representatives were often required to bargain in uniform, were required to salute and come to attention before entering the negotiations, and were forced to sit (if at all) at the far end of a long table from the commissioners. While the attitude of the employer varies from one board to another and while acceptance of parity is still the exception rather than the rule, the extreme intimidation and patronizing attitudes have disappeared. What remains is annoying, but does not really inhibit collective bargaining. The police associations are agitating against a present practice of having commissioners (particularly judges) serve on the commissions of several municipalities, and have indicated that they find the presence of judges awkward altogether. Until the nature and composition of the commissions are reformed, however, there will continue to be inhibitions on effective collective bargaining.

At present most police contracts signed in Ontario are annual agreements, although a few are two-year contracts, and a small number extend over three years. Because of the essential similarity of the contracts and because they come up for renegotiation at different times, a "leap-frog" syndrome inevitably develops which creates pressure on board and association alike. These developments have led to the de facto pegging of the terms of the contracts signed by the smaller boards to the trends set by the larger boards and by the OPP. Increasingly contracts negotiated across the province have become almost identical and actual centralization of bargaining is a likely prospect. In the future this trend can be expected to become even more noticeable and will further diminish the ability of local boards to hold out for atypical terms or to intimidate local police associations. As a result of a 1969 amendment to the Police Act, arbitration awards will be enforceable as if they were court judgments. This provision will quickly bring into line recalcitrant municipalities who have failed to implement awards promptly.

One further problem which arises out of the collective bargaining procedure deserves mention. In police labor relations as in the private sector, the rights of each party are normally derived from the collective agreement and vindicated through a grievance procedure, culminating in binding arbitration. Yet municipal councils may pass bylaws which affect the police but are beyond the reach of either negotiation or the grievance procedure. Two comparatively recent examples illustrate this problem. In one community, controversy developed over the issuance of a traffic citation to a commissioner. He succeeded in having the municipal council pass a bylaw which in effect stated that if necessary a police commission could overrule a member of the police force in the enforcement of traffic offences. In another community, a municipal bylaw was enacted which provided that police who lived further than a stated distance from the town would no longer be employed. Attacking such provisions probably involves going to the OPC, but up to the present the OPC has not been notably sympathetic to the cause of the police. With the expected closer control over the OPC by the provincial government, it is hoped that the situation may change.

A TALE OF TWO CITIES: TORONTO AND MONTREAL

Collective bargaining between the largest single police force in Canada and Metropolitan Toronto over the last five years has been characterized by incredible delays, marked reluctance on the part of the employer to tolerate interference by either association or arbitral tribunal in what it considers to be management prerogatives, and by mutually acrimonious relations. These tensions stem from a number of causes. The police association is articulate, is prone to challenge the views of the employer in fields which, a few years ago, were management's exclusive preserve, and has shown a skilled understanding of the use of the press to achieve its ends. The upper echelons of the police force achieved their positions by rising through the ranks in an earlier era and have little patience for what they seem to perceive as the "dictates" of mere constables. In addition, their relations with the press have been less than happy. Finally, the police commission is dominated by appointed personnel who are well into their second decade of service and who find the altered conditions difficult to accept. These problems exist to a greater or lesser degree throughout most of Ontario, and perhaps are highlighted in Toronto because of the size of the force and the complexity of the problems. For these reasons it will perhaps be useful to survey the Toronto problem at somewhat greater length.

As of August 1969 the last collective agreement fully implemented between the MTPA and the police commission was that relating to 1965-66. The annual negotiations for 1967, 1968, and 1969 had all ended in arbitration awards. The 1967 award gave rise to a closely contested grievance which is not yet resolved; the 1968 award was subject to two further grievance arbitration decisions which have recently been handed down. The 1969 award published in the summer of 1969 was characterized by a bitterness seldom found in arbitration hearings.

While specific aspects of each award will be considered, two general comments are applicable to all three years. The MTPA has focused upon the desire of the public for an efficient and honest force, and has consistently maintained to the press that unless the police were granted even higher increases, the quality of the force would suffer. At negotiation time, reports of resignations appear in the press as "proof" of the need to increase wages and improve working conditions. However, to what extent these resignations represent normal attrition and to what extent they are a function of low morale is only conjecture. Second, the insensitivity of police management to the trends which produced a strong police association is quite remarkable. As in some other areas of private and public employment, the employer has been unable to accept the bargaining representative as a partner in working toward tolerable industrial relations. In private industry the fact of collective employee action is accepted, albeit sometimes reluctantly; in this particular area of public employment the employer has seldom shown a full understanding of the impact which the existence of collective employee action must have on its operations.

Negotiations for the year 1967 went to arbitration in August and the arbitration award for 1967 pay rates was announced only on October 20. The award was a good one for the police, who received a 15 percent increase. Moreover, of great symbolic significance, the board of arbitration rejected a request by the commission for the deletion of a clause in the existing collective agreement which gave special leave of absence to P. C. Brown, the president of the MTPA, and preserved his status as a full-time member of the force. Since the police association had to be represented by a full-time police officer, if the commissioners' request had been granted it would have forced a severe curtailment in the work of the association. The request has been repeated annually since 1967, and rejected with regularity, but is symptomatic of the insensitivity of the commission to current realities in police employment.

The same award included a clause which significantly affected the rotation of shifts and which was a clear victory for the association. However, this clause has still not been implemented, because the employer maintained it could not do so. The association eventually sued to compel compliance with the award. Although it received a judgment to the effect that the award was binding, and that the board of arbitration had acted within its jurisdiction in relation to the particular matter, relief was denied because the association had not exhausted the compulsory arbitration mechanism established for grievances under the Police Act.[25] Currently, the appointment of an arbitrator by the attorney-general is awaited.

This requirement of "double arbitration" is bitterly attacked by the police, who feel that they should not have to invoke a second arbitration proceeding in order to compel the commission to comply with an (allegedly) unambiguous award issued in the original arbitration over the terms of the new contract. At a minimum their resentment is justified by the fact that municipalities are in a position to delay interminably the implementation of unpalatable awards. Once a dispute has been arbitrated, the police maintain, a second arbitration is redundant. This criticism, of course, misses the distinction between the original "interest" arbitration and the second "rights" arbitration.

Negotiations for the 1968 contract began in March of that year, and on April 19 the MTPA gave notice that it was going to arbitration. The dispute went to arbitration on September 26, and a result was promised by November 26; the award for 1968 was finally published on December 12. This excessive delay was due in part to the six weeks or so it took to appoint all the arbitrators, but the primary cause was the heavy case load with which the arbitrator, Judge Deyman, was saddled. The long delay and the small (6 percent) increase awarded combined to shatter police confidence in the system and to inject a more militant note into the 1969 negotiations. Once again the award was not implemented fully and two clauses were the subject of grievances which had to be processed through to arbitration. One matter in dispute, relating to pensions, was decided in July 1969, while the decision in the other was pending months later. In the pension award the board stated: "the operative provisions of the award are clear and unambiguous." Even though the decision was not unanimous, a reading of the 1968 interest arbitration award and the 1969 grievance arbitration award suggests that the original meaning was clear and there should have been no necessity to go to another board for further interpretation. The 1968 award was contested by the commissioners for tactical reasons and because of an intense reluctance to accept binding decisions on certain matters submitted to negotiation and arbitration.

The "slow ritual of negotiation" concluded somewhat earlier in 1969, and by July 17 an award had been published. The majority of the board dealt chiefly with the salaries issue and awarded a pay increase of 15 percent. The bitter dissent of the commission's nominee stated "ad hoc arbitration boards with incompetent chairmen are not the answer to compulsory arbitration," and concluded: "it is most difficult for me to believe that the Board was either judicial or impartial."

Two other disputes enlivened public interest in police problems in 1969. The first was the refusal to give the MTPA any representation on the committee which oversees their pension fund investment. The three Metropolitan Toronto Police Benefit Fund trustees now include the metropolitan chairman and finance commissioner and the police commission chairman. An overwhelming percentage of the police pension fund is now invested in low-interest municipal bonds, and police association attempts to alter this pattern have met with no success. A second controversy was triggered by the publication of a photograph of the president of the MTPA sitting in his uniform and holding out a tin cup; P. C. Brown had a sign around his neck reading "give generously." The picture accompanied an article highly sympathetic to the police association and was published before the 1969 arbitration was announced. The commission reacted by declaring that Brown would be disciplined for bringing discredit upon the reputation of the police force. However, after much adverse public reaction, the charge was withdrawn when Brown agreed to turn in his uniform; he was permitted to retain his leave-of-absence status and his police identity card.

This brief recital of the problems of the Toronto police illustrates that management-labor relations within the police forces is not yet completely "normalized." Perhaps in time, as the police association and the commission establish some modus vivendi, problems of this type can be expected to vanish. To repeat what has already been stated, most of the difficulties appear to be a function of the novelty of genuine labor organization among the police and the inability of a conservative management to react with any sort of understanding to this strange phenomenon.

The Montreal story is far more dramatic and recently was punctuated by one of the few police strikes in North American history. The strike—which also embraced most of Montreal City's 2400 firemen—lasted for 16 hours, from 8:00 A.M. until midnight of October 7, 1969. Quebec, like Ontario, provides a system of compulsory arbitration for the resolution of collective bargaining impasses involving public safety employees. More explicitly, the Labour Code provides: "Strikes are prohibited in all circumstances to the police officers and firemen in the employ of a municipal corporation."[26] Why, then, did a strike occur in the teeth of such a prohibition?

The stoppage appears to have been provoked by the failure of an arbitration board to place Montreal police on a position of wage parity with their Toronto counterparts. In prearbitration bargaining, the police had requested an increase of $1900 for 1969-70, which would have placed them at the Toronto level; the arbitrator awarded them an increase of $730 for 1969 and $400 for 1970, which left them $1100 behind Toronto for 1969 (with the possibility of a bigger gap in 1970 as the collective agreement in Toronto terminates on

December 1, 1969). The policemen felt this margin was totally unacceptable. Moreover, a major nonmonetary demand made by the police was decided against them by the arbitrator. For some time the police had wanted patrol cars to carry two men. The chairman of Montreal's executive committee had driven around town in a police cruiser to judge for himself if this was necessary; he decided one man was enough, and the arbitrator agreed. Tragically, only two days before the strike a Toronto policeman was killed while on solitary patrol. This event reinforced the conviction of the Montreal police that the arbitrator had not sufficiently considered the safety considerations of two-man patrols, and it added emotional fuel to the crisis.

The events of the strike appear to justify the gloomiest predictions of those who are adamant about the denial of the right to strike to public safety employees: an on-duty policeman was killed during a riot and a burglar was shot by a citizen defending his home; there were 61 armed robberies (including 6 banks); $2 million-worth of windows was smashed, and an additional $1 million damage done by rioters in the downtown area.

At 5:00 P.M., after the strike had lasted almost 8 hours, the Montreal police and those of adjacent municipalities were placed under the command of the provincial director of police, and by 9:00 P.M. approximately 800 provincial policemen also arrived in the area to assume public security functions. A regular army regiment was also called to the scene at the request of the provincial government. The striking police reacted by "hijacking" eight of the provincial police cruisers and jamming the provincial police communications network.

Finally, late that night Quebec's National Assembly unanimously passed Bill 61 ordering all striking policemen back to work by 12:01 A.M. the following day. Penalties were provided in the act for noncompliance of (1) up to $100 a day and jail for up to a month for individual strikers, (2) between $5000 and $50,000 a day and up to one year in jail for union leaders, and (3) decertification of the union if 70 percent failed to return to work by Wednesday.

Under the threat of these drastic consequences and having vividly dramatized their complaints, the police (and firemen) returned to work as ordered.

Yet the strike does not prove the proposition that police will strike recklessly, merely because they fail to gain their bargaining objectives. The stoppage and its consequences can only be understood against the special background of Montreal and the social and national ferment of the province of Quebec.

Barely two decades earlier, in 1946, the Montreal police had struck over the basic issue of the right to bargain collectively. Emerging out of this strike, the Montreal Police Brotherhood had managed to provide fairly effective representation and until recently had secured its objective of wage parity with Toronto. However, in 1967 a subparity settlement was accepted as part of a general civic appeal to avoid labor disputes during Expo 67. Disaffection created by this settlement was compounded by several unilateral management moves in 1968 and 1969, including suspension by the city of its 11 percent pension contribution for two years and initiation of efficiency programs without prior consultation. Finally, during the 1969 negotiations the city did not condescend to make any counteroffer to the police wage proposal or even to suggest an appropriate increase to the arbitrator. The folly of this position was implicitly admitted when, following the strike, the city agreed to an increase greater than that provided by the legally binding arbitration award. Thus blame for the strike, at least in part, can be found in the city's conduct.

However, the city's financial position must have been at least partly responsible for its negotiating posture. Overextended as a result of its Expo program, faced with financial difficulties due to the effect of the separatist crisis upon investors, Montreal also shared the frustration of many urban municipalities at having to pay the cost of policing without contribution from its suburban neighbors, who could afford to make do with small local police forces. Shortly after the strike a new cost-sharing arrangement was introduced, and shortly thereafter a new scheme proposed for the integration of all services in the metropolitan area, as well as its police reorganization.

However, other cities have suffered financial difficulties and provocative police managements without experiencing a strike. The Montreal situation contained additional ingredients unique to the Quebec scene, yet somehow related to America's current urban crisis. Foremost among these was the problem of French-Canadian nationalism, which was manifest in several respects. First, Montreal has experienced student and separatist riots and demonstrations in recent years, which inevitably have left a wide breach between the police and the public. Second, the goal of wage parity with English-speaking Toronto was more than economic; it represented a new awareness—and resentment—of the fact that French-Canadians in Quebec have generally been less affluent than English-Canadians in the neighboring province of Ontario. Third, the economic difficulties of Quebec had over the past few years created considerable labor discontent, particularly among public service workers. Government intransigence confronted employee impatience. Indeed, within a matter of days prior to the police strike, there had been illegal strikes of employees in hospitals and the provincially owned Hydro Quebec, as well as several groups of school teachers. Thus the police strike was in a sense the next "logical" step. Fourth, even the major incidents of rioting and violence were connected with the French-Canadian identity crisis, as an anarchist-separatist group of taxi operators chose the occasion to demolish the buses of a non-French company which enjoyed a monopoly over the lucrative airport transportation service. In all of these ways, then, the special political problems of Quebec made the police strike more than a mere labor problem.

Less capable of precise definition is the effect of a general crumbling of traditional authority in Quebec in many other walks of life, which must inevitably affect even such instruments of authority as the police. In religion, in education, in social customs, in politics, the new Quebec has tended to slough off the restraints of the old. The resulting social tensions must not only have impaired the public image of the police, but must have weakened police discipline as well.

For all of these reasons, then, the Montreal experience cannot be viewed as a basis for predicting what will happen, for example, in Toronto (although it may be analogized to some racially tense American cities).

DISCIPLINE AND THE GRIEVANCE PROCEDURE

As will be evident from the foregoing account of the Toronto situation, the Police Act stipulates that "differences . . . relating to the interpretation, application or administration" or violation of a collective agreement, or of an (interest dispute) arbitral award may be submitted to final and binding arbitration. The arbitrator's award may be registered in the Supreme Court and enforced as an order of the court,[27] and is binding upon the municipal council and the police commission.[28]

However, collective agreements do not govern matters of discipline which are the subject of regulations made by the provincial cabinet under the Police Act.[29] This code of discipline applies to all police forces in the province and provides an elaborate mechanism for the adjudication of "charges" relating to major and minor offenses. In the case of the former, the code proclaims a right to counsel, the opportunity to make full defense, and a series of appeals from a hearing officer to the chief of police, then to the police commission, and ultimately to the OPC. Minor offenses are dealt with on a less formal basis, but the same ultimate appeal is provided, although only with leave of the OPC itself.

The regulations also contain an elaborate list of substantive offenses, variously categorized as follows:

1. Discreditable conduct
2. Insubordinate or oppressive conduct ("insubordinate by word, act or demeanour")
3. Neglect of duty ("idles or gossips while on duty")
4. Deceit
5. Breach of confidence ("canvasses . . . any person in respect of a matter concerning the police force . . . or calls or attends any unauthorized meeting to discuss any matter concerning the police force")

6. Corrupt practice
7. Unlawful or unnecessary exercise of authority
8. Damage to clothing or equipment
9. Consuming intoxicating liquor in a manner prejudicial to duty
10. Lending money to a superior
11. Borrowing money from or accepting a present from any inferior in rank
12. Gaming

To this list (of which only the major headings have been cited) are liable to be added regulations made by particular police commissions. Small wonder that the PAO complained: "no other group of citizens in Canada are subject to the unjust principle that is inherent in these regulations. No other police force in Canada or the United States has such a code of discipline. We are not desirous of the distinction of being the only law enforcement agency in Canada to operate under a system that would have been antiquated fifty years ago."[30]

As has been noted, the entire subject of discipline—and especially the central role of the management-oriented OPC—is now under review. The Ontario police forces may well stand at the watershed between their paramilitary traditions and a new era of bilateral, private-sector style industrial discipline.

CONCLUSION

The influence of the Ontario system may well be widespread in the years to come. On its own merits the system has much to recommend it. Through a difficult period of evolution, the police have managed gradually to achieve a reasonable measure of fair dealing in their relationships with their employers. Except in the area of discipline (and perhaps even there, in the near future) institutions now exist in Ontario for the resolution of disputes and the effective adjudication of controversies which should do much to accommodate the tensions and pressures of career policemen under difficult contemporary conditions.

Perhaps there is significance in the fact that the International Conference of Police Associations (ICPA, with which most American police are affiliated) recently elected as its president P. C. Brown, the president of the Toronto police association. Brown made this prediction:

> Strange as it may seem, the Canadian police officers have had and will have a greater effect on American forces. In the United States very few, if any, police organizations enjoy the right of free collective bargaining and compulsory arbitration. Ontario police associations have enjoyed this right for at least 25 years.
>
> Without proper collective bargaining and compulsory arbitration rights, police officers are faced with only two alternatives—one of political lobby, which leads to many undesirable consequences; or of uniting with organized labour for the purposes of strength and power. Neither of the foregoing alternatives are desirable, nor are they wanted by the overwhelming majority of American and Canadian police officers.
>
> Under our newly rejuvenated ICPA, we hope to provide the guidance and assistance that will provide for the adoption of model legislation, similar to the Police Act of Ontario, for all Canadian and American police officers.[31]

Whether this fairly restrained position will prevail in the face of more extreme elements within the police ranks will probably be determined by the speed with which governments come to accept the necessity for "normalization" of police employment. At the moment, Brown's position is probably an accurate description of police sentiment:

> [N]o police officer wishes to become a part of the trade union movement, and I sincerely believe that the trade union movement and trade unionists themselves realize that police officers cannot affiliate with them and still enforce the law fairly and impartially. Police officers hold organized labour in high esteem and recognize the vital part it plays in our society. I trust that organized labour recognizes

and appreciates the role police officers must play in their daily chores on behalf of all citizens of every community.[32]

However, in some other jurisdictions some police are already turning toward unionization and away from the ICPA. Unless the ICPA is able to bring reasonable satisfaction to its affiliates through some such model as Brown proposes, this trend may well accelerate.

·V·

The Informal Public Sector Model: Collective Bargaining in the Public Service of Ontario

THE collective bargaining system of the Ontario public service is undergoing significant, perhaps fundamental changes. In the recent past it could fairly be characterized as a process of informal consultation; today formal negotiation and grievance procedures have been developed which culminate in third-party adjudication; tomorrow the remaining institutional vestiges of the precollective bargaining era may be dispelled by the growing militancy of dissident groups who seek normal employer-employee relationships of the private sector type.

These conclusions differ from the predictions—and recommendations—of a recent public inquiry by Judge Walter Little into the Ontario system,[1] but they are based upon trends in public and private sector employment relations in Ontario and elsewhere. The significance of the divergence may become apparent from an examination of the present system and an analysis of Judge Little's report.

THE LEGISLATIVE FRAMEWORK: FROM CONSULTATION TO NEGOTIATION

The Province of Ontario first enacted legislation regulating civil servants in 1878 when the Public Service Act[2] was passed designating the lieutenant-governor in council (the provincial cabinet) as the controlling agency in the service, with authority to classify the civil service and to hire, promote, and dismiss employees.

Little change occurred until 1918, when a civil service commissioner was appointed to investigate and make recommendations regarding possible departmental changes, civil servants' salaries, appointments, departmental complaints, and civil servants' behavior.[3]

In 1947 a new Public Service Act was passed establishing a Civil Service Commission.[4] The commissioners, appointed by the lieutenant-governor in council, examined candidates for the service, certified candidates' qualifications, and assigned them to a classification with salary. Only after this was done could the candidate be appointed to the service. While this important reform helped to displace patronage in the public service and to lay the groundwork for a developing professionalism, it did not resolve the fundamental shape of employer-employee negotiations. Indeed, until 1963 "negotiations" is a misnomer since there was no formal vehicle for the resolution of controversies in the provincial public service over wages and working conditions. The only forum for discussion between the government and its employees was a Joint Advisory Council comprising three representatives of the Civil Service Association of Ontario, three government representatives, and one member of the Civil Service Commission who acted as chairman and cast a deciding vote (on procedural matters). The Joint Advisory Council was, as its name implies, basically a medium of communications through which civil servants might transmit their collective views to the government. Its decisions were not binding on the parties and its effectiveness was severely limited. However, the council did establish a mechanism to deal with individual employee grievances, initially an informal, nonbinding procedure under the aegis of the Civil Service Commission, latterly (since 1959) an effective impartial adjudicative tribunal.

The basis for formal negotiations was ultimately established by the Public Service Act of 1962 and elaborated in a series of amendments throughout the 1960s.[5] In essence the system presently envisages direct negotiations, mediation, and compulsory arbitration of interest disputes. However, certain institutional weaknesses coupled with external pressures led to a decision that the system should be thoroughly reviewed. Accordingly, as indicated, Judge Walter Little, an experienced labor mediator, was appointed special adviser for this purpose and between July 1967 and May 1969 undertook a survey of the act and its operation.

THE MANAGEMENT FUNCTION IN THE ONTARIO PUBLIC SERVICE

The province's public service may be divided into two main categories for present purposes—those which fall under general private sector labor relations laws and those which do not. In the former category are employees of such independent agencies as the Hydro-Electric Power Commission of Ontario and the provincially owned Ontario Northland Railway. However, the great majority of the 51,000 employees of the provincial government, employed both in the central administration and in various "crown agencies" (other than those enumerated above),[6] bargain under the Public Service Act.[7] Thus the Public Service Act covers an enormous variety of white- and blue-collar workers, primarily in Toronto—the provincial capital—but also in the most remote corners of the province.

Management responsibility for employment relations is vested formally in the Treasury Board, a permanent cabinet committee with a permanent staff, whose wide duties and powers relate to the control of public monies. In August 1964 the government established the Staff Relations Branch of the Treasury Board to represent it in negotiations. The director of the Staff Relations Branch is the chief negotiator for the official (management) side, and he, together with two assistants from his own branch or seconded from the Civil Service Commission or other departments (depending upon the matter in dispute), make up the management negotiating team.[8]

The Public Service Act assigns to the Civil Service Commission responsibility for its administration.[9] The commission is to comprise not fewer than three persons, one of whom may be appointed chairman. It has the assistance of a full-time staff, constituting the Department of the Civil Service, which provides the commission with the information needed to perform its duties. These are varied: job classification, salary range recommendations (subject to the negotiation procedure), recruitment, assignment of persons to classified positions, determination of perquisite changes, staff development programs, and reporting upon the performance of its duties. Most commission decisions are made after examination of classification and pay data developed by the Department of the Civil Service. Decisions are then referred to the Treasury Board to be put before the cabinet prior to implementation, which obviously signifies that the commission enjoys something less than plenary power and complete independence. In effect the Civil Service Commission is an executive arm of the Ontario government with some functional autonomy in the area of personnel administration. Clearly it lacks the hallmarks of true impartiality which would enable it to perform the third-party function in collective bargaining and impasse resolution.

ORGANIZATION OF ONTARIO GOVERNMENT EMPLOYEES [10]

The Civil Service Association of Ontario, Inc. (CSAO), is recognized by implication in the Public Service Act as the official spokesman for the main body of public service employees in Ontario.[11]

The CSAO has slowly developed from a "tame" social organization to an independent association which has demonstrated some degree of militancy in pursuing its economic objectives. Indeed, within one year after its formation in 1911, the association's activities had expanded to include discussions with the government regarding working hours and superannuation. In 1920 the Civil Servants' Superannuation Plan was established, and the association was officially recognized as representing civil servants with the right to nominate to the Superannuation Board.[12] As might be inferred from this initial recognition of the CSAO, during the early years the association and the government apparently maintained a happy if somewhat incestuous relationship: association representatives met with the premier and cabinet members, and senior government officials were members of, and held office in, the association.

In 1920 the association was incorporated under the laws of the Province of Ontario. In 1944 further formal recognition was given the CSAO when a Board of Review and Joint Advisory Council were established, with association representation, to discuss employment benefits and security.

As in most clubs, association dues were paid in cash.

However, recruitment and maintenance of membership became an increasing problem as the size of the civil service grew. This problem was somewhat alleviated in 1950 by the government's decision to permit voluntary revocable deduction of membership dues from pay.[13]

Membership in the CSAO now stands at approximately 33,000.[14] Each member is assigned to one of 178 branches, comprising 26 geographical districts, each of which selects a member of the CSAO board of directors. The board determines the association's policy pursuant to its mandate from the membership.

The president is on full-time leave of absence from government employment, and the association reimburses the government for his salary and other costs. This device is intended to protect the CSAO and the government from suggestions of management domination while maintaining the long-term employment rights of the president against the hazards of electoral defeat. To carry on its daily business, the association employs approximately 40 full-time employees, headed by a general manager. He also acts as chief negotiator, with the assistance of two other staff members, and is otherwise a preeminent figure in the formation and advancement of CSAO policy.

As noted, the whole role of the association has undoubtedly undergone change. Its orientation is no longer social; its aims and objectives are economic in nature. Inevitably the CSAO has had to become more concerned with membership participation and to make efforts to involve members in the negotiation process as participants, advisers, or at least observers. This growth in militancy and activity has been particularly marked since 1967 and recently led to the appointment of an internal study group to examine deficiencies in the organization and to suggest areas of improvement.[15] What has caused this upheaval?

In part, of course, the general mood of labor militancy in Canada[16] since the mid-1960s has pervaded the Ontario public service, reflecting the impact of upward trends in expectations, private sector wages, and the cost of living. But more particularly, the new posture of the CSAO can be explained by events within the public service, particularly a series of threats to its virtual monopoly of representation. In several instances the provincial government assumed responsibility for services formerly under the control of municipalities or of some semiautonomous agency whose employees had been organized by other unions, principally the Canadian Union of Public Employees. On another occasion an institution which had been directly administered by the province was established as an independent university (the University of Guelph), and the CSAO had to protect its position by seeking certification under the private sector Labour Relations Act. Again, several dissident groups within the public service proper, dissatisfied with the quality of CSAO representation, have sought to impugn its authority as their bargaining representative.

By and large the CSAO has beaten back these challenges. To what extent its success reflects genuine membership loyalty, to what extent an artificial advantage based on special statutory status, must next be explored.

DETERMINING ISSUES OF REPRESENTATION

The Public Service Act establishes no procedure by which bargaining units may be defined or bargaining representatives selected. Indeed, to the extent that questions of representation are dealt with at all, the statute effectively precludes employee choice by according a favored position to the CSAO. It is this organization alone[17] which has the right to nominate "staff side" representatives to the bodies involved in collective bargaining and arbitration under the act. To a very slight degree, however, the severity of this principle is mitigated in practice by the existence of separate bargaining units in a few anomalous crown agencies, described below.

This exclusive prerogative of representation has attracted strong criticism. For example, the Canadian Union of Public Employees (CUPE)—supported by editorial opinion—claimed that it should continue to be the bargaining agent for a group of jail guards and court clerks whom it had represented prior to the provincial assumption of direct control from their former municipal employer.[18] At the level of principle, another provincial inquiry in New Brunswick which sat at the same time as the Little inquiry likewise favored democratic choice of bargaining representatives: "If an association represents a majority of employees in a bargaining unit it should not object to the establishment of procedures that would test the reality of its claim."[19]

In agreeing that employees should be granted freedom of choice in the selection of a bargaining agent, Judge Little recommended the establishment of a procedure to allow initial choice (and discontinuance) of collective bargaining representation within an established bargaining unit where the majority of the unit so desires. To ensure this freedom, he recommended that an independent adjudicator should be appointed whenever the occasion requires, to deal with the issue on the basis of applicable private sector criteria and principles.[20]

This recommendation, however, even if implemented, is unlikely to have much effect upon the CSAO's preeminent position for several reasons.

First, the CSAO had been the beneficiary of a voluntary checkoff under which it managed to attract approximately 56 percent of those eligible for membership in the central administration. But, it complained that this practice was unfair and burdensome, since nonmembers are often new employees, part of the rapid employee turnover, who wish simply to escape the cost of membership. In keeping with this reasoning CSAO suggested that all employees who benefit from the negotiations conducted by their bargaining agent should pay dues to the association in order to defray the costs which bring them benefits. Moreover, the association contended, compulsory checkoff would reduce wildcat action since the association would have greater control over all employees. While union security is relatively common in the private sector and might be justified on this basis, the argument relating to the reduction of wildcat actions in the public service is hardly persuasive: wildcat actions are both infrequent and ineffective in the public service and, in any event, had recently been directed at the CSAO itself.

Judge Little's report recommended that there should be

automatic monthly deduction of dues for new employees and for employees presently having dues deducted, and that there should be deduction upon written authorization from all other present employees. However, he also recommended that the revenue thus produced "should not be used for purposes other than those directly applicable to all members of the respective bargaining units."[21] Within a few months after the Little Report was received, the government moved to institute a compulsory dues checkoff, as recommended, subject only to a novel exclusionary formula for conscientious objectors.[22] The effect of this move is to render the CSAO virtually invulnerable to displacement.[23]

A second key factor in the entrenchment of the CSAO is the current (and proposed) configuration of bargaining units in the Ontario public service. There is no statutory provision governing the composition of bargaining units. Presently the principal unit, Public Service-Civil Servant (Classified), includes such classifications as unskilled and skilled, inside and outside employees, clerical staff, hospital attendants, and professionals. Moreover, this unit bears no particular relationship, in terms of size, to any other unit, as is revealed by the following list of existing bargaining units:[24]

Public Service—Civil Servants (Classified)	43,733
Ontario Provincial Police	3,395
Liquor Control Board and Liquor Licence Board	2,626
Ontario Hospital Services Commission	250
Ontario Water Resources Commission	
Head Office	455
Plants	208
Niagara Parks Commission	
Administration	180
Police	15
Ontario Housing Corporation	
Maintenance Staff	260
Total	51,122

Thus it is clear that while there is little community of interest within the major bargaining unit, it is so large and geographically dispersed that there is little likelihood of its capture by another union. Moreover, the few existing beachheads such as the Ontario Housing Corporation (organized by CUPE) and the Liquor Control Board (organized by a break-away employees association) were the result of historical an-omolies and offer little prospect as a jumping-off point for invasion of the entire service.

Surprisingly, Judge Little recommended maintenance of the existing province-wide bargaining units: "the public interest is best served if the public service is not fragmented by the introduction of new units which would give rise to multiple bargaining where the need is not apparent."[25] Which "needs" Judge Little considered is not difficult to infer. As he suggests in discussing the right of employees to select their bargaining representative, the problem of unit definition is intimately connected with that of choice of representative,[26] and the incumbent CSAO can hardly fail to benefit from his recom-mendation. Moreover, Judge Little's preoccupation with the potential diversity of conditions engendered by a multiplicity of units likewise indicates his recognition of government's need for managerial convenience and efficiency. But of the "need" of employees for self-determination and autonomy, there is little perception.

Indeed, the present all-encompassing unit of 43,000 em-ployees is so unworkable that the parties, by agreement, bargain separately for each of its five constituent occupational categories. At a minimum it is difficult to see why this arrangement could not be institutionalized so that the present single bargain-ing unit is subdivided into five. By contrast, some of the existing smaller units can hardly be viable, nor can they be justified on any grounds relating to their distinctive functions.

In the light of these considerations, Judge Little's refusal to even contemplate the possibility of future changes in the bargaining unit, or to recommend any means whereby future controversies might be decided, may well justify the prediction that this issue will remain in the public arena for years to come.

The identification of persons appropriate for exclusion from the bargaining process has been a problem. Under the present system it has been resolved by negotiation between the departments or agencies of government and the CSAO and, failing agreement, by the Civil Service Commission.[27] Judge Little commented that negotiations at the departmental level resulted in lack of uniformity across the public service in the excluded positions and classes, and recommended that criteria for exclusions be adopted and applied along job classification lines, without regard to departmental boundaries. The need for clearer criteria of exclusion based on managerial or confidential functions was recognized even by the CSAO, which would stand to lose a number of existing prestigious members high in management ranks.

The move toward the industrial type bargaining automatically forces upon the Association the exclusion from the bargaining unit of members who formerly under the old type of consultative system were not only allowed to be members, but welcomed as members as was their participation in bargaining procedures. A number of exclusions have already been negotiated or decided and the Association must face up to the fact that it cannot, on the one hand, have industrial bargaining rights and procedures and, on the other hand, continue some of the paternal arrangements.[28]

Judge Little observed that the parties had generally agreed that the "level of exclusions in the public service should be higher than in the private sector" since "public service managerial authority is not always delegated to junior levels to the same extent as in private industry" and, furthermore, authority delegated to a classification is not always fully exercised by the incumbent.[29] He also agreed in general with the government's proposals, based on private sector criteria such as management and supervision functions, policy-making, budget formulation, confidentiality, and short-term or part-time employment.[30] It was hoped that this approach would make for a more formal and effective bargaining relationship with a sharper division between management and nonmanagement personnel.

One group, professional employees,[31] provided Judge Little with special difficulty. His report adopts the professional exclusion provided for in the private sector Labour Relations Act: members of the architectural, dental, engineering, legal, and medical professions entitled to practice in Ontario and employed in a professional capacity. In addition, the range of professionals to be excluded from collective bargaining was to be greatly expanded by the addition of those possessing the following characteristics: (1) a university degree awarded after a four-year course in a specialized field; (2) the government of the profession is a recognized governing professional society formed under the provisions of a provincial statute; (3) the profession provides a specialized and skilled service to a client which cannot lawfully be obtained from other groups, usually on a fee for service basis rather than as salaried employees; and (4) a clear community of interests among the persons concerned. At a time when professional employees in the private sector and in the federal government are moving militantly toward collective bargaining, implementation of these recommendations may give rise to some problems.

Given the special relationship of the Civil Service Commission to the government and its statutory obligation to make the initial classification of employees,[32] it is clear that some other body must possess ultimate authority to decide questions of inclusion or exclusion from the bargaining unit. Here again Judge Little turns to the device of an independent arbitrator, appointed ad hoc.

NEGOTIATIONS

The Public Service Act defines the scope of bargaining as "any matter concerning the terms of employment of Crown employees, including working conditions, remuneration, leaves and hours of work, that is not excluded by the regulations."[33] In the major bargaining unit, in practice, bargaining is divided into three main phases: rates of pay, fringe benefits, and other matters relating to general working conditions and terms of employment. The Department of Civil Service and the CSAO have established a cyclical review system, pursuant to which they review salaries every two years at staggered intervals for each of the five classifications in the unit. Fringe benefits are negotiated for all classifications at one time but independently of salary negotiations. The third area of discussion, working conditions, may be local in nature (e.g. holiday schedules) and negotiated between management and employees at the departmental level. However, where working conditions relate to such items as overtime, hours of work, and grievance procedure, negotiations are conducted by the CSAO and the government on a service-wide basis.

This third category provides some difficulty in regard to the level at which negotiations should be conducted. Regulations passed under the act[34] make provision for the establishment by the Civil Service Commission of a system of departmental councils (and branch councils within departments) to secure administration-staff cooperation and to suggest improvements and encourage utilization of staff ideas. These councils were to be composed of equal numbers of members, one half appointed by the minister of the department and one half elected by the civil servants in the department or branch. In practice, local problems were discussed at council meetings and occasionally resolved, but the parties were unhappy with the councils and complaints of management domination were soon heard. They are now being replaced by a system of direct negotiation between the CSAO and the departmental deputy minister or his nominee. However, problems persist. Each department interprets matters as being local, and therefore within its competence, in a particular way; some departments claim more autonomy than others. This could result in less uniformity across the civil service than might be desired, although to date the parties do not consider that local negotiations have had this effect.

More seriously, the separation of negotiations into three distinct phases would appear to inhibit the collective bargaining process by not allowing the parties to trade off a gain in one area against a concession in another.

The CSAO submission to Judge Little requested that there be only two bargaining packages, namely rates of pay and all other conditions of work (including fringe benefits). It also requested that the scope of bargaining encompass all matters which might subsequently become a part of the working conditions as a result of management action. For example, one of the strongest sources of annoyance to the CSAO has been the administration of the Public Service Superannuation Act under which the employer and employee each contribute to a fund. The government is able to vary the benefits from those which obtained at the time of the individual's initial employment, decide how the employees' contributions should be invested, the rate of interest to be paid, and the accrual of eventual benefits. The CSAO maintains that pensions are a condition of work and that an employee should have a proper voice, through his bargaining agent, in the fate of his salary deduction.

However, Judge Little apparently felt that management should continue to enjoy unilateral decision-making powers in certain areas and accordingly found that there must be matters which are to be excluded from the scope of bargaining.[35] His report recommended that departmental organization, complement, classification, job evaluation, the merit system, and superannuation be excluded from bargaining. He further suggested that provision should be made for uniformity in mileage rates, allowable expenses for moving on transfer, commuting and weekend allowances, and similar matters which should be applied universally to all employees, whether members of the bargaining unit or not. This restriction, no doubt, will be a spur to continued militancy.

Prior to the commencement of negotiations, benchmark jobs are selected for preliminary examination by CSAO and Department of Civil Service experts. Because there are so many classes of jobs in each occupational group, and because many of them are peculiar to government service, the two sides place great stress on the attempt to reach mutual agreement as to benchmarks. Generally benchmark jobs possess a significant number of incumbents, have an identifiable relationship with other classes within the service, and are characterized by content and qualifications which can be matched with similar jobs in the private sector; if the parties cannot assign a benchmark to a class of jobs, it will be dealt with separately in negotiations. The parties then negotiate on the benchmark jobs, beginning with an exchange of initial positions and attempting to reach an agreement without third party assistance.

In preparation for negotiations the Pay Research Bureau of the Department of Civil Service conducts a cyclical salary review. About 30 to 60 days prior to meeting with the CSAO, the bureau submits its recommendations on salary revision to the director of staff relations, who then presents the recommendations to the Treasury Board. Treasury Board, after discussion with the director and the Civil Service Commission, establishes limits within which the director may conclude an agreement.

Normally the government's pay policy is to relate the third quartile of rates outside the public service to the maximum within, and the first quartile outside to the minimum within. Thus an Ontario civil servant should be in a position where, if all the persons in the province performing comparable jobs were ranked as to earnings, only 25 percent would receive higher remuneration than he. The CSAO apparently accepts this third quartile target as realistic,[36] and in theory the area of bargaining should therefore lie between the two parties' analyses of what they perceive to be the third quartile.

Implicit in this account is the fact that the CSAO and the government each develop different statistics, although when the parties explore benchmark jobs to be negotiated, they normally agree upon a list of specific classifications and the numbers of employees in those classifications. By way of explanation, the association claims that the government relies too heavily on the published job specifications which are often not currently descriptive, rather than factual knowledge of the actual job performed.

Clearly, then, the difference in research materials used by the parties underlies much of the failure to reach agreement. Further difficulties arise from the parties' different interpretations of the same facts and the differences in value placed upon such factors as mobility and security of tenure. Possibly some of the differences could be resolved by the establishment of an independent pay research bureau supported by both parties, as exists at the federal level. However, neither party seems particularly interested in seeking an independent bureau, both stating that data and information supplied by it would be subject to different interpretations. As a result, the CSAO maintains its own Pay Research Department which recommends to the association's board of directors that certain salary revisions are in order, as the basis of the employees' negotiating position.

Conceivably, increased sophistication at the ultimate stage of arbitration or tensions produced by the interaction of government cost-consciousness and employee militancy might produce a future willingness to develop a common factual framework for negotiations.

A further complication results from the fact that the parties do not presently negotiate on a regular basis a single package of economic benefits and working conditions. Rather, they are in theory free to reopen any issue at any time, and in fact they do discuss a variety of matters at different times. In order to regularize and expedite the bargaining process, Judge Little recommended that the parties give four months' advance notice of the commencement of negotiations, including details of proposed amendments and additions. The requirement of a notice period will necessitate some changes in the parties' research procedures, which will now have to be geared to regular periodic review. Although this rather practical problem of reorganizing research data could result in short-term problems, the parties consider that it will result in earlier finalization of agreement.

As indicated, the parties begin negotiations with direct discussions at the expert level and then move to a direct meeting of the negotiating teams. If no settlement is reached during direct negotiations, either side may request that the chairman convene a meeting of the Joint Council.[37] By statutory requirement, the Joint Council consists of three members appointed on the recommendation of the Treasury Board ("official side"), three members appointed on the recommendation of the CSAO ("staff side"), and a nonvoting chairman, all appointed by the provincial cabinet. In its early years the employer representatives on the Joint Council were all deputy ministers (the senior civil servant in a department). Hence negotiations concerning matters affecting the entire public service were negotiated primarily at meetings of the Joint Council, with the result that deputy ministers were spending a great deal of time in negotiations rather than looking after the affairs of their own departments. Hence the "official side" membership of the council was revised and now comprises the director of staff relations (Treasury Board) and the executive director and director of pay and classification standards (both of the Department of Civil Service). The "staff side" is represented by the CSAO president and two of its full-time employees. Although there is no statutory provision requiring the parties to agree on the appointment of the chairman, it appears that the incumbent, A. R. Dick, deputy attorney-general, has received the approval of both sides, despite his "management" identification.

The act requires that the chairman, at the request of either or both sides, shall place on the Joint Council agenda any matter concerning the terms of employment of crown employees which is not excluded by the regulations. The significance of being "placed on the agenda" is that a duty to negotiate is thereby created.[38] Thus the chairman by his control over the agenda has the power to determine the scope of bargaining under the act. No doubt assignment of the chairmanship to a high government official would not be workable were it not for the fact that the legislation enables either party to require that a matter be placed on the agenda. In fact, the parties have controlled the agenda through the vehicle of a steering committee.

More importantly, the early experience of the Joint Council demonstrated the need for other avenues of discussion. By establishing preliminary procedures to define, narrow, or settle issues prior to Joint Council consideration, the parties have recently been able to clear its agenda.[39] Simultaneously, however, they have managed to create an informal bargaining process which in effect has preempted the statutory system. In practice, few issues are now actually resolved by the Joint

Council, which tends merely to send unresolved disputes on to the next step.

The CSAO has urged that the Joint Council, instead of being used as a formal body of referral, could be used more profitably to decide such matters as the methods and procedures to be employed in research.[40] Judge Little appeared satisfied with the present system and recommended that the Council "continue as presently constituted and, particularly, as a forum for the discussion of matters which are neither negotiable nor subject to arbitration, but which are of mutual concern to the government and its employees. This will serve as a useful medium for the development of better communications between Management and Staff."[41]

Should the negotiations at the Joint Council stage result in agreement, this fact is evidenced by the execution of a written document, signed by the senior members of each side, which is transmitted by the chairman "to the appropriate authority to be implemented."[42] But as indicated, the usual inability of the parties to resolve their differences at the Joint Council merely moves the dispute to the next step in the process: intervention of a mediator on the appointment of the minister of labour.[43]

Generally the parties consider that mediation is a useful step for it allows them to reach mutually agreeable settlement without the imposition of a third-party decision. However, there is some suggestion that mediation delays settlement since the parties may be unwilling to move from their positions because of a belief that ultimately an arbitration award may place them in a more favorable position. It appears that this risk is diminished by the fact that parties may divulge private feelings and ideas in confidence to the mediator without fear of disclosure to the other side and thus may retain collective bargaining positions while continuing negotiations through new avenues of approach suggested by the mediator.[44]

Mediation was used twice in early 1967 and was successful in respect of one important round of negotiations affecting some 10,000 employees. On this occasion the CSAO experimented with employee participation by submitting the government offer, obtained at mediation, to the association members in a secret ballot ratification vote. This was the first time that there had been direct membership ratification of a salary offer.[45]

If mediation fails, the next—and final—step is arbitration. The arbitration board, appointed by the provincial cabinet, comprises a chairman appointed for a renewable term of two years and two members, one appointed by the official side of the Joint Council and one by the staff side.[46] The arbitration board conducts hearings prior to handing down a decision, a copy of which signed by its chairman, is transmitted to the chairman of the Joint Council, who transmits it to the appropriate authority for implementation.[47] In providing that an arbitration award shall be implemented, the statute clearly contemplates that the board's decision will be final and binding upon the parties. Implicitly, too, although the act does not expressly prohibit strikes, the binding nature of the arbitration award seems to make it clear that such action is not contemplated.

Given the finality of its award and the relative inexperience of the parties with negotiation, mediation, and arbitration, it is perhaps inevitable that the initial tendency of the arbitration board was to engage in informal conciliation rather than pure adjudication. However, as the process has evolved, there is a discernible trend for the parties to adopt a strictly adversary posture before the board. Whether this trend, reflecting and exacerbated by growing employee militancy, will permit the question of strikes to be dealt with by mere inference is doubtful.

THE RIGHT TO STRIKE

Up to the present there has been little controversy within the Ontario public service on the issue of whether employees should resolve bargaining impasses by the use or threat of strikes. The present statute neither expressly prohibits nor expressly permits strikes. Both the government (predictably) and the CSAO have indicated their satisfaction with the present system. Two recent inquiries into Ontario labor relations—the

Rand Commission (concerned with labor disputes in general) and Judge Little's inquiry—have recommended against the legalization of strikes in the public service.

The Rand Report urged: "When individuals or groups voluntarily undertake these responsibilities [of public employment] they enter a field of virtual monpoly; the community cannot secure itself against rejection of those responsibilities by maintaining a standby force which itself would be open to a similar freedom of action."[48]

Judge Little considered the problems relating to the right to strike in the public service and similarly concluded that such a right should not be permitted in Ontario. First, he noted that the two parties did not object to the present practice and that it appeared to have operated satisfactorily and effectively. Second, Judge Little considered the problem at the level of principle, as an illustration of the democratic dilemma of conflict between individual and community interests. In our society, he said, when a representative is elected to govern we consider that there is a duty placed upon him to provide the community with a continuity of governmental operations. Judge Little considered that public service employees should therefore not be permitted to withdraw their services with the objective of preventing a duly elected government from discharging this duty and forcing it to meet employee demands. He stated:

> Governments are elected to formulate policies and to make decisions for the benefit of the whole community. No individuals in the community, and particularly those who are employed to ensure, and are actively engaged in, the effective implementation of such policies and decisions, should be able by concerted action, to impede or frustrate such implementation in order to enforce their will on the citizens as a whole.[49]

In reviewing Judge Little's recommendations, the CSAO reiterated a rather Delphic position, which it had initially taken in its submissions to him. Silence in legislation regarding the right to strike is desirable, contended the CSAO, providing that government recognizes the need for impartial arbitration and that arbitration boards fulfill their duty of providing equitable awards. The association claimed that *"There must be no direct prohibition of strike.* The right must be reserved for employees to discard arbitration as the final step if it proves to be unfair, inequitable or biased towards the employer."[50] This statement would seem to suggest that the employees consider that if legislation is silent in regard to this matter, they now have the right to strike as an ultimate recourse. If this is indeed true, the provisions making compulsory arbitration final and binding might be rendered meaningless.

Despite the CSAO position, and despite an explicit request from the government for an articulated ban on strikes, Judge Little refrained from suggesting any change in the status quo. Rather, he contented himself with admonishing the association that "the sovereignty of the state must remain supreme" while reminding government of its correlative obligation "to ensure that those who are not accorded the right to strike are rewarded for their services on a basis at least as favourable as those who have such right."[51]

In every respect the position in Ontario evokes memories of the federal government situation in 1965 following the report of the Heeney Committee:[52] strikes are neither legalized nor forbidden; government favors a prohibition while the major employee spokesmen oppose it; and forces beyond the immediate relationship seem likely to determine the issue in the long run—and perhaps the short run. In 1965 the postal workers' strike forced immediate reconsideration of the whole problem by all parties and, in effect, shifted the main body of federal public employee opinion from hostility to acceptance of the strike. In 1970 in Ontario there is also an "outsider" union, CUPE, which favors a federal-type statute with a right to strike for provincial public employees. However, its strength is isolated in one small bargaining unit. More importantly, there are dissident groups within the all-embracing core bargaining unit who feel that their interests and identities have been submerged. These groups on several occasions have threatened, or engaged in, wildcat strikes. The Little Report recommendations on the preservation of this unit make it almost inevitable that there will be continuing unrest and extralegal self-assertion in the form of work stoppages. If these become sufficiently widespread or frequent, the issue of legalizing their conduct will once again have to be confronted.

THE AGREEMENT

Although the Public Service Act contemplates that "every agreement reached [by the two sides of the Joint Council] shall be put in writing and ... signed,"[53] it cannot be said that the statute envisages the execution of collective agreements of the private sector style. Rather, agreements reached at the bargaining table or at mediation, and arbitration awards, take effect through amendments to the Ontario Regulations, through orders-in-council, or through directives issued by the Treasury Board, the Civil Service Commission, or the relevant departmental officials.

The association expressed its disapproval of these provisions to Judge Little. The present act offers no safeguard against unilateral government action of this very sort which would alter conditions of work without prior negotiation or agreement between the parties. The CSAO therefore suggested that future changes in working conditions, however announced, be negotiated and agreed upon prior to implementation. It was further suggested that if all conditions of work, other than pay, were handled as a single package at negotiations, and agreement reached, these should be incorporated in a signed agreement as in the private sector. However, agreements concerning rates of pay would have to be implemented by order-in-council.[54]

It is hard to defend the present system. Apart from the patent unfairness of permitting government to act, and appear to act, unilaterally in areas which are committed to bilateral determination, the piecemeal implementation of negotiated or arbitrated wages and working conditions is inefficient. To determine what actually has been agreed to, and what should be (re)negotiated, it is necessary to cull literally dozens of official documents to gain a complete picture. Judge Little firmly recommended the execution of formal collective agreements covering all matters in negotiation and lasting for a fixed term of at least one year and preferably two.[55]

GRIEVANCES

Regulations[56] passed pursuant to the Public Service Act divide grievances into three areas: dismissal, working conditions and terms of employment, and classification. A Public Service Grievance Board composed of not fewer than three members (one of whom is chairman) appointed by the provincial cabinet is the final authority for all matters other than classification. A Classification Rating Committee, consisting of at least three persons designated by the chairman of the Civil Service Commission, provides the final stage for classification grievances.

In the case of a dismissal a grievor may apply to the Public Service Grievance Board for a hearing within twenty-one days of receiving a dismissal notice. A hearing is conducted by the board, which then renders a final decision and reports to the minister and deputy minister concerned, sending a copy of the report to the grievor and his representatives.

In cases relating to working conditions and terms of employment the grievor may present a complaint informally to his immediate supervisor within fourteen days after he has become aware of his complaint. If informal discussion does not result in satisfaction, the grievor may present the supervisor with a written complaint within seven days. The supervisor has then seven days within which he must render a written decision, from which, within a further seven days, the grievor may appeal to a person designated by the deputy minister for the purpose, and if this is unsatisfactory, ultimately to the deputy minister himself. The deputy minister must conduct an investigation into the grievance within fourteen days of the date of presentation and render a written decision within seven days thereafter. Most importantly, the grievor has ultimate recourse to the impartial Public Service Grievance Board, which has power to render a final and binding decision after conducting a hearing.

Where the grievor alleges that he has been wrongly classified, he advises his supervisor and requests that the grievance be referred to the deputy minister, who must investigate and give a written decision within twenty-one days of presentation. Appeal lies within seven days to the chairman of the Civil Service Commission, who refers the grievance to the Classification Rating Committee. Hearings are held within fourteen days and a binding decision is rendered by the committee.

Certain points should be noted in relation to the legislation and regulations governing grievances. First, the grievance procedure is not restricted to public servants within the bargaining unit. The regulations extend to all persons who are employed in the public service under the jurisdiction of a deputy minister for a certain period of time, with limited exceptions. Second, the regulations provide that if the interpretation of any legislation, regulation, or rule relevant to a grievance is disputed at a hearing, the Public Service Grievance Board or the Classification Rating Committee may request the attorney-general for a written opinion. Third, no provision is made for a bargaining agent to bring policy grievances; a grievor may present a grievance personally or be represented or assisted by an employee representative, but nothing permits the CSAO to take the initiative in presenting a grievance. The CSAO has attempted to lessen the effects of this provision, however, by arranging for an individual to file a "test grievance." For example, the CSAO recently solicited grievances from members to test the validity of an official directive which provided that only persons actually employed in positions on the effective date of a salary revision would automatically qualify for higher pay. The association argued on behalf of employees hired after the effective date of the salary adjustment that the arbitration board which ordered the revision had intended that salary ranges should apply to classes of employees, and that no employee should be entitled to enter into nonconforming individual agreements with management in matters covered by the arbitration award. The Public Service Grievance Board acknowledged the grievances as test cases and ruled in favor of the employees.[57]

The greatest problem in the area of grievances concerns

the volume of cases and the resulting backlog and delay. One possible way of alleviating this situation would be to increase the numbers of board members in order to facilitate more sittings by different panels of the board, which has a quorum of two. A further suggestion concerns the right of an employee to bring his grievance personally. Normally an employee takes his complaint to the association; after investigation the association advises him whether it considers he has a valid grievance. In the event that it considers his complaint valid it generally acts as his representative, giving him the benefit of its professional staff. However, if the association considers that his complaint lacks merit or reasonable prospect of success, it may refuse to act as his representative. Nonetheless, he may proceed to present his grievance to the board personally. Possibly the number of grievances would be reduced if employees were obliged to accept the determination of their bargaining agent, although the price paid in terms of individual rights might be excessive. Here again the federal precedent may be worthy of examination: employees have the right to grieve against discipline but otherwise must accept the determination of their bargaining agent.

Apart from the problems of volume and delay, the parties seem relatively pleased with the present system. Grievances are successful in approximately one third of the cases, a figure quite consistent with private sector experience. Apparently "the trend of more settlements at the lower levels of procedures is continuing as is the trend for fewer decisions in favour of the grievor at the final level."[58] This observation is consistent with the view that the grievance procedure relating to working conditions should not be subject to sweeping changes as parties frequently resolve matters prior to adjudication by the board.

Some problems have arisen in regard to classification, although their source is not the malfunctioning of the grievance procedure, but rather the attitude of government which continues to maintain that classification is a unilateral management prerogative. Generally, decisions respecting the establishment of new classifications, or the restructuring of old classifications, are made unilaterally by the government without consultation with the CSAO, which is only notified after the event. However, in some instances the government advises the association of a change after the classification has reached the formative stage but before the classification is made effective, and asks for comments. This request comes a little late if it is genuinely intended to produce a meaningful response; its usefulness is only in providing the association with some forewarning of classification reorganization or creation. The burden of this criticism is reduced only to the extent that relief against arbitrary classification of particular individuals may be sought through the grievance procedure, although the new classification, per se, is unimpeachable.

Judge Little recommended that the Classification Rating Committee be continued because it preserves consistency in the administration of the evaluated salary structure, which applied to employees both inside and outside the bargaining unit. However, as to other kinds of grievances, he suggested that the existing procedure should be replaced by a formal grievance procedure established under each collective agreement. Provision should be made, he urged, for final and binding arbitration of grievances resulting from the interpretation, application, or alleged violation of the collective agreement's terms.[59]

CONCLUSIONS

Ontario public employees have been traditionally quiescent. Only in the past ten or twelve years has significant pressure been exerted on the government to establish a procedure for collective bargaining. This phenomenon is a result of several factors, many of which are found in other North American jurisdictions, some of which are peculiar to Ontario.

In the early history of the province the public service consisted of only a few hundred men and women, many of whom were employed, at least indirectly, as a result of political patronage; they were not likely to be ungrateful or aggressive. As the public service grew in size and professionalism, this group dwindled in size, but the atmosphere in the public service was probably influenced by the attitude of its early members. Furthermore, Ontario has had prolonged periods of one-party domination of the legislature, and it has been suggested that "members of the Civil Service are found equating the government with the majority party instead of servants of the administration."[60] Again, this attitude is likely to produce servility. Finally, the only group providing representation for these employees until recently has been the CSAO, an association whose raison d'etre was originally social. The movement toward collective bargaining, therefore, has been in part a movement for the internal transformation of the CSAO.

The CSAO, however, has matured into an agency with economic aims. Recently its position has been challenged by other unions, and recommendations, however unworkable, have been made to allow employees freedom of choice in selecting a bargaining agent. This has forced the CSAO into a more aggressive posture vis-à-vis the government and has led to greater membership involvement in negotiation procedures. Most importantly, the civil servant's self-image has undergone changes. No longer is his position based on patronage, no longer does he concede that security of tenure is an acceptable substitute for reasonable wages. He has seen his federal counterpart assert rights denied to him and will not long be content to accept a lesser status.

The wave of interest and the increasing activity of provincial employees has, however, not resulted in sweeping legislative change. Rather, change has been slow and fragmentary, and the Little Report does not presage a more vigorous pace of reform. Presently the two major parties to collective bargaining, the CSAO and the government, appear content with the status quo, as evidenced by their submissions to Judge Little. Although both parties raised contentious issues, neither complained so loudly as to make sweeping change necessary. Obviously it is in the government's interest to have only a single, semimilitant employee representative to bargain with and obviously the CSAO wishes to be that representative. Thus each party bolsters the other's position by maintaining that the present system is flexible and workable.

To the outside observer the present system, while workable, hardly provides other jurisdictions with a suitable model for change. While many of the problem areas have received comment from Judge Little and have already been dealt with in this paper, it is perhaps beneficial to summarize a few of the most obvious.

First, the fact that negotiations are conducted separately in three areas—wages, fringe benefits, and working conditions—results in rigidity in bargaining due to an inability to set off items against each other. Second, the maintenance of pay research departments by each party encourages disagreement in regard to criteria used in obtaining information and data. Third, bargaining at local or departmental levels, while encouraging employee participation and enabling employees to become conversant with negotiation procedure, could result in a lack of uniformity across the civil service. Fourth, mediation's effectiveness is impaired by the delay resulting from the necessity to first place matters on the agenda of the Joint Council. Fifth, interest-dispute arbitration has suffered from the tendency of the arbitration board to conciliate rather than adjudicate. As the parties have become more firm in their positions, and as negotiations have become much tougher, the board is increasingly required to redefine its role and act as a true arbitrator. Finally, there is the absence of collctive agreements. Directives, orders-in-council, and amendments to regulations provide no substitute for a bilateral agreement. The interested employee would have a difficult task should he wish to understand the terms of employment negotiated on his behalf.

Thus we see the Ontario system in a transitional phase, with the Little Report recommending limited changes within the context of the present system in order to formalize and regularize it. However, just over the horizon there appear to be forces which may ultimately displace the present system and force it into the public-private mold developed at the federal level.

·VI·

The Professional Model: Collective Bargaining in the Ontario Schools

C OLLECTIVE bargaining by teachers in many Canadian provinces has developed rapidly within one of the several conventional "models" canvassed above. However, collective bargaining in Ontario's school system presents a paradox: although educational policy and administration are undergoing profound, perhaps revolutionary changes, although education has ranked highest on the list of municipal and provincial spending priorities, Ontario teachers participate in collective bargaining through institutions which resemble medieval guilds.

The guild model, the model of the self-governing profession, is not restricted to the educational field. (The Ontario legal profession no doubt represents the paradigm which has been emulated by the teachers and by other groups.) In brief, the self-governing profession (as its name implies) enjoys a monopoly on the rendering of a service and a mandate to ensure that those who render such service conform to appropriate standards of competence and ethical behavior. However, the profession's discharge of its mandate remains largely immune from public control, though not, of course, from public criticism.

In the power of the profession to exclude nonmembers from competition and in its virtually unfettered control over its own members reside the strengths of a potentially invincible bargaining agency. Yet, strangely, a second paradox, there is little evidence that the Ontario teachers have utilized this power. Perhaps it is the "professional" image which has so far imbued its members with a sense of self-restraint; perhaps it is the realities of the educational labor market which have led to the establishment of an operative "informal public sector" system of collective bargaining and have somewhat displaced the formal statutory regime; perhaps it is the relative affluence of the Ontario school system and the relative liberality of its educational philosophy which have so far avoided recourse to the confrontations and conflicts which are increasingly frequent elsewhere. Whichever of these explanations may be accurate, it seems clear that there is a new militancy abroad among Ontario teachers. Will the professional model be able to contain this new militancy, exacerbated as it may be by predictions of a shift in public spending priorities and of a parental backlash in matters of educational philosophy? The answer to this question may be suggested by the analysis that follows.

THE STRUCTURE AND GOVERNMENT OF THE ONTARIO SCHOOL SYSTEM

Responsibility for overall educational policy in Ontario resides ultimately in the provincial minister of education and his department.[1] Province-wide standards of teaching are achieved through provincial certification of teachers; basic curricula and course outlines are developed by the provincial authorities; extensive research in educational methods has been undertaken by the Ontario Institute for Studies in Education; and important financial assistance is given by the province, through a variety of programs, to local educational authorities.

But important power, especially in relation to collective bargaining, is also vested in a system of elected county and municipal school boards.[2] Prior to 1968 local boards of education existed in hundreds of towns and villages. However, under provincial direction a process of integration and rationalization has now produced a much smaller number of more viable educational constituencies, largely organized on a county basis, except in the municipality of Metropolitan Toronto, whose particular arrangements will be canvassed below.

Responsibility for employment of teachers and negotiation of salary levels and other benefits is vested in these school boards. So too, to a large degree, is responsibility for raising the financial resources needed to pay these and other educational costs. Each school board annually prepares an estimate of revenue required for the succeeding year. This estimate is submitted to the municipal council, which is obliged to raise the required sum by levying a tax assessed on real property. If the municipality also wishes to make a special grant for school purposes it may levy a further tax. However, an increasingly important source of financing for elementary and secondary schools is the provincial government's Ontario Tax Foundation Plan. This plan provides two types of subsidies for school boards: a dollar grant based on student attendance and a percentage grant relating to certain approved costs. Furthermore the government may pay an "equalization" grant to certain boards, the purpose of which is to maintain a minimum level of education throughout the province, and a "stimulation" grant to encourage boards to provide special services beyond the essential minimum. Finally, "growth-need" grants are available where capital costs are higher than the provincial average, and "attendance growth" grants are paid where the area is rapidly expanding and a board must suddenly increase services in the school.

The situation in Metropolitan Toronto is somewhat different. The six local boards of education (one for each of the six constituent Metro municipalities) have varying tax bases upon which to raise money for education since tax is levied on real property values which are not uniform throughout the entire area. These area inequalities resulted in pressure to spread the cost of education (and thus the quality of education) evenly throughout Metropolitan Toronto by means of one common tax structure. Accordingly, the Metropolitan Toronto School Board was created in 1953 to ensure equal education opportunity for Metro children and was given ultimate responsibility for educational finance when the Metropolitan Toronto Act was overhauled in 1966.[3] Under the present system each of the six local boards prepares an estimate of monies required for the coming year, which it submits to the Metro Board. The Metro Board receives and examines each budget and discusses its contents with local staff and board. The budgets are compared and local priorities are established; adjustments may then be made to ensure that available funds are fairly apportioned to the six areas. After this process is completed the Metropolitan Toronto School Board submits a single composite budget to the Metropolitan Council, and it is at this level that a uniform rate is set for Metro and incorporated in local tax bills.

As will be appreciated, even on the basis of this brief survey, there exists a delicate balance between central and local authority over educational policy, and between central and local responsibility for educational finances. Although there seems to be a general decentralizing trend in the policy area in favor of the newly strengthened county and municipal school boards, it seems inevitable that responsibility for educational costs will move increasingly to the provincial government. The strains generated by these opposing tendencies are bound to be reflected in the collective bargaining process.

Ironically, although education is a massive, complex, expensive phenomenon involving massive teacher recruitment, school site acquisition, design, care and maintenance of structures, curriculum determination, administration, and a host of other functions, the right of teachers to bargain collectively is based almost entirely on traditions and nonstatutory, extralegal procedures. Although expressly denied the right to organize, bargain, and strike under the provincial Labour Relations Act,[4] teachers have nonetheless developed a viable collective bargaining system under the aegis of special legislation relating to their professional organizations.

TEACHER PROFESSIONAL ORGANIZATIONS [5]

The teachers of Ontario first organized on a provincial basis in 1918-1919 when the Federation of Women Teachers Associations of Ontario (FWTAO), the Ontario Public School Men Teachers Federation (OPSMTF), and the Ontario Secondary School Teachers Federation (OSSTF) werè established. In 1935 the three federations formed a loose coordinating body, the Ontario Teachers Federation (OTF). Accomplishments were few and the bargaining position of the three federations was weak, largely due to the nonrepresentation of certain groups of teachers and to the absence of any form of compulsory membership. Between 1939 and 1944, however, the remaining groups became organized, and pressure mounted within the ranks of the teachers to establish a coordinating body.

In response to these demands the government enacted legislation in 1944 conferring upon the OTF extensive powers to regulate the teaching profession. By virtue of this legislation every teacher in Ontario must belong to the OTF, while even students in teachers colleges or in colleges of education must hold associate memberships.[6] The act also provides that school boards must deduct membership fees from the teachers' salaries either annually or in installments and remit these to the federation treasurer. The OTF in turn remits a percentage of the fees collected to each of the affiliated organizations on a per capita basis, each affiliate having previously fixed a fee based on the amount necessary to carry on its work. This system of compulsory membership and checkoff gives the OTF, and more particularly its affiliates, both enormous power and access to considerable financial resources.

The OTF board of governors, comprising forty members who are affiliate representatives, is responsible for policy-making and consultation with the provincial department of education. The executive, a nine-member body, effectively discharges OTF business and directs the staff employed at the head office in Toronto in performing routine day-to-day tasks. However, although the board of governors is ostensibly responsible for determining policy, important developments are only discussed initially at board meetings. They are then referred to each of the affiliates for discussion and approval prior to being voted upon by the board of governors. If one of the affiliates objects to the proposed policy it may register its nonconcurrence two weeks subsequent to the board of governors' meeting, thus preventing adoption of the proposal as OTF policy.[7] The existence of this veto power, coupled with a requirement that all OTF members also be members of a constituent organization, shows where the real power lies: clearly it is the affiliates which have de facto control over policy, and it is they which claim the primary loyalties of teachers.

The five affiliates[8] are also provincial organizations with elected executives. Each is divided into several regions or districts which in turn have branches, units, or locals with elected local executives. Each affiliate is an autonomous body which establishes its own policy and provides special services such as sickness benefits, legal advice, and publications. However, jurisdiction over disciplinary matters is shared by the federation and the five affiliates, the affiliates' discipline committees having jurisdiction only over cases of minor importance.

OTF policy also requires that each affiliate should establish and maintain a "relations committee" to deal with cases of unethical and unprofessional conduct. The affiliate is required to refer the matter to the OTF's relations and discipline committee if the matter is sufficiently serious. More specifically, those relations and discipline cases dealing with broken contracts, a question of morals, or a breach of the code of ethics (formulated in 1944 and now, in revised form, included in the regulations under the Teaching Profession Act) are to be referred directly to the OTF by the affiliates and dealt with at that level at first instance.[9]

The OTF Relations and Discipline Committee consists of two representatives from each affiliate. When the president of the OTF receives a report of unprofessional or unethical conduct he refers it to the executive which may refer it to the Relations and Discipline Committee for its opinion. The committee notifies the accused and the affiliate of the time and place of a hearing at which it will consider their submissions. If, following a hearing, the accused is judged to be guilty on a simple majority vote, the committee may recommend such penalties as it deems appropriate within the authority of the regulations passed under the Teaching Profession Act. The committee then conveys its decision to the executive and to the accused, who may appeal first to the executive and ultimately to the board of governors, a hearing being conducted in each instance. If the committee's decision is sustained, the executive or the board may then reprimand the teacher, recommend to the minister that he suspend the member's teaching certificate, or suspend the member from the OTF subject to the minister's consent.[10]

This power over the professional status and livelihood of all teachers (subject only to ministerial control) is of obvious importance in the assertion of collective power; the individual defies the majority only by risking his entire career. To date this procedure has not been resorted to in the context of collective bargaining.

ORGANIZATION ON THE EMPLOYER SIDE

The strength of the teacher organizations and the increasing pressure exerted by these bodies resulted in some boards of education forming school trustee associations. In 1950 seven of these associations formed a loose affiliation, the Ontario School Trustees Council. The council maintains a permanent Toronto office and gives assistance to school boards involved in bargaining in the form of statistical comparisons and reports of other negotiations and settlements. The council's activities are not extensive and it does not participate directly in the bargaining process unless specifically requested to do so. As noted, salary determination is the responsibility of each local board, and assistance is more likely to be sought from the affiliated trustee association than the council.

School boards have frequently complained that they are weak in comparison with the teacher associations. This complaint is compounded by the fact that boards have been forced to compete with one another in their recruitment of teachers in what has been, until very recently, a sellers' market. Furthermore, trustees have no real vested interest in the outcome of negotiations. The pressures exerted upon them are political in nature rather than financial, and their experience at the bargaining table may be somewhat more limited than the teachers whose associations provide them with training in negotiation. When twenty-five boards in southwestern Ontario organized for "coalition bargaining," because the teachers had allegedly been playing one board off against another during negotiations, the teachers objected strenuously. The teachers contended that school boards represent a particular district, and that joint action for purposes of negotiation constituted a failure to serve their own district residents. However, despite these objections school boards have continued to press for more cooperation and joint bargaining. As noted earlier, it seems clear that financial pressures will produce strong pressures for centralization.

BARGAINING UNITS

The size of the school district normally determines the configuration of bargaining units, keeping in mind that each comprises at least two units, the secondary school teachers and the elementary or public school teachers. The former group is represented by the OSSTF, generally regarded as the most powerful representative body in the teaching profession, and the latter by the FWTAO and OPSMTF. The two elementary school federations frequently bargain jointly, since few male teachers teach at the elementary level and their power as a single group would not be strong. They cooperate in salary discussions and form a central bargaining committee composed of an equal number of men and women teachers.

Probably one of the striking aspects of teacher negotiations is the inclusion of principals, vice-principals, and department heads in the same bargaining unit as classroom teachers. The Teaching Profession Act includes these people as members of OTF, and the associations accordingly bargain on their behalf as part of the general bargaining unit. Understandably, school boards have opposed the present practice and sought to exclude principals, as part of management, from the "union" side, as in the private sector. In some instances this approach has been adopted, and school boards have been able to insist upon negotiating with principals individually or through a representative principals' committee.

It has been suggested[11] that principals in Ontario have limited administrative powers, do not enjoy responsibility for teacher evaluation, dismissals, transfers, and recommendations for probationary or permanent appointments. These factors, together with the principals' membership in the "teaching team," might perhaps provide justification for their inclusion in the unit.

No doubt the inclusion of the principals in the employee organization does make for more effective employee representation. Pressure by the OTF and by the affiliates to retain the principals in their ranks, and in the unit, stems largely from the fear that effective leadership in the organizations and in the negotiations will be lost if principals should be excluded. At present, principals are active participants in negotiations and hold leading executive positions in local organizations. Since teaching is a mobile profession, with many women leaving the labor force at least temporarily, there is a great need for a stable, constant cadre of association members. Principals, career-orientated and with obvious administrative ability, provide this stable influence and the leadership necessary to maintain strong associations.

However, this would not seem to provide justification for their continuing inclusion in the unit. The principal has obvious administrative functions, and his inclusion in the unit results in a division of his loyalty between the association and the school administration. Examination of the Ontario school principal's statutory duties shows that he is, among other things, responsible for the maintenance of order and discipline in the school. He must furnish the minister of education and school inspectors with information regarding the "condition of school premises, the discipline of the school, the progress of the pupils and any other matters affecting the interest of the school."[12] More importantly, in practice he often takes the responsibility of interviewing prospective teachers and recommending their employment to the school board. Thus although final, formal responsibility for hiring a teacher lies with the school board, practical responsibility lies with the school principal. His duties are wide and the position he occupies is one of responsiblity involving much administrative decision-making. To the extent that normal industrial relations precedents are relevant, the arguments for exclusion seem strong. No doubt increasing teacher militancy will force some ultimate resolution of this issue.

NEGOTIATIONS

Since the Teaching Profession Act establishes no formal negotiation mechanism for teachers and school boards, the procedure which has developed is a melange of practice, precedent, convenience, and informal agreement.

As has been indicated, the act requires OTF membership and establishes a compulsory dues checkoff for all teachers. However, the OTF requires that each of its members also be a member of one of the five affiliates, so that each teacher in Ontario has a dual membership and is represented at the bargaining table by one of the affiliates. The bargaining procedure employed by each differs slightly, since there are no prescribed statutory arrangements. However, certain general themes can be identified.

Each local of an affiliate initiates negotiation in its district by serving notice on the appropriate school board. Each district executive normally has the responsibility of selecting a team of negotiators to bargain with a committee of school trustees. The teachers' team is usually representative, consisting of a principal or vice-principal, department heads, and teachers. The negotiators generally have authority to reach a tentative agreement which they will subsequently present to the local for ratification. Power to make binding commitments without need for ratification by the membership is granted to negotiators in some cases, especially in rural areas. This practice has resulted in strong criticism by some OSSTF members who feel that the strength of the association depends on member participation.

In the event that a local is unable to resolve a dispute, it may request the assistance of its provincial association. If this should be the case, a staff officer from the provincial association becomes involved in the negotiations. While he may meet with the school board's committee or a representative from a trustee association, and is sometimes authorized to contract on behalf of the teachers (usually subject to membership ratification), generally the staff officer plays a less obvious role, merely assisting the local with its bargaining, giving advice and making suggestions to local negotiators. In fact, the provincial associations are seldom involved in direct negotiations with school boards, but their presence is felt in most negotiations as a result of activity behind the scenes.

To date neither the teacher associations nor the school boards have employed the services of professional negotiators in collective bargaining. The teachers have registered strong objection to any third-party presence at the bargaining table, maintaining that only educators can understand teachers' problems and concerns.

If settlement is not forthcoming despite the intervention of the association, representatives of the two central provincial bodies—the OTF and its school board counterpart, the OSTC—may intervene in negotiations. If their informal mediation fails, and if a local contemplates making an "in dispute" designation, the penultimate sanction described below, a special advisory committee, may be established. This committee, comprising an equal number of teachers and trustees not involved in the dispute, meets with the parties and makes settlement recommendations. Perhaps predictably, the success of such committees has been severely limited since their recommendations are not binding. Indeed, some of the associations fail to recognize their existence or to employ their services.

RESOLVING IMPASSES

Until recently there had been no attempt to invoke third-party or neutral assistance in resolving bargaining impasses. Of course in the absence of any legislative framework for negotiations, there was no convenient means for invoking either mediation or arbitration except for the mutual commitment of the parties to such a procedure. However, the teachers had resolutely rejected third-party intervention.

Some slight change in attitude toward third-party intervention was indicated in early 1969, when for the first time the Metropolitan Toronto School Board and the Toronto Secondary School Teachers agreed upon the appointment of a mediator. Happily, the 1969 experiment was considered to be successful. While the parties continue to be opposed to compulsory methods of resolving impasses, they may well come to accept voluntary introduction of a third-party catalyst to settlement on a regular basis.

When negotiations break down completely the local may decide to issue an "in dispute" designation, advising teachers of a bargaining impasse with a particular school board. Variously described as a "pinklisting" or a "graylisting," these letters warn present and prospective teachers that if they should accept a teaching position within the designated area they may lose association privileges and protection. As an ultimate sanction the OTF may effectively "blacklist" a recalcitrant school board by invoking regulations made under the Teaching Profession Act which provide that "a member shall . . . refuse to accept employment with a board of trustees whose relations with the Federation are unsatisfactory."[13]

Blacklisting would be used only under extreme circumstances such as the refusal by a school board to recognize or negotiate with an affiliate. Should a teacher fail to comply with an affiliate's gray- or pinklisting and accept employment with a school board subject to an "in dispute" designation, the affiliate may react by suspending or expelling him. This action, however, does not result in the teacher being prevented from teaching providing OTF membership, required under the act, is maintained. Normally the OTF regards the graylisting as being a matter internal to the affiliate, and it will not follow the affiliate's lead in suspending or expelling the teacher. While the OTF bylaws do provide that a teacher must maintain membership in an affiliate, an exception is made "in cases where the membership has been suspended or cancelled in an affiliated body."[14] Thus the effectiveness of the graylisting is potentially limited and a teacher in fact may not be prevented from practicing his profession for failure to comply with an affiliate's warning.

If, however, the OTF blacklists a school board and a member accepts employment in contravention of the OTF prohibition, he may lose his OTF membership. He would thus be in breach of the Teaching Profession Act, which requires every teacher to be an OTF member, and the OTF would request the minister of education to cancel the certificate of the "offending" teacher. Whether he would do so is politically problematical; whether he can legally refuse is doubtful.

Graylisting has met with varying degrees of success. In one case a suburban Toronto school board reacted to a graylisting by requesting the other school boards in Metropolitan Toronto to refrain from hiring its recalcitrant teachers until a settlement was reached. The board hoped to maintain a static state in which it could negotiate without fear of losing teachers to other boards in the area. The OSSTF claims, however, that this retaliation was ineffective as other boards, desperate to obtain teachers, failed to comply with the request. The effectiveness of this method of countering the teachers' weapon would appear to depend on the labor market for teachers. In general, since until very recently there has been a sellers' market, school boards rightly fear the "in dispute" designation as a potent weapon.

Blacklisting has, in fact, been resorted to infrequently. However, in Toronto in 1967 the school board reacted to the OSSTF pinklisting by threatening to hire retired teachers. The OTF then entered the dispute, supporting the OSSTF, and recommended that neither active nor retired teachers should accept a position with the board. Such action by the OTF, while unusual, had the result of forcing prospective "proemployer" teachers to risk explusion from both groups, and consequently loss of professional status. Undoubtedly it was the risk of such dire consequences which ultimately led the parties to settle their differences.

While a blacklisting virtually amounts to a threat to strike by ensuring that no teachers will continue in employment upon expiry of their current contracts, it is different in the sense that no actual cessation of work is contemplated before that date. In fact there is no legislation prohibiting strike action by teachers. Mass resignations, however, are the preferred formula. Teachers' contracts provide that notice of termination (other than by mutual consent) may be given in writing by either party to take effect on either August 31 or December 31 of any year.[15] These provisions allow the associations to organize mass resignations of teachers to take effect just before the fall or spring academic sessions, which would effectively close the schools. To all intents and purposes this amounts to strike action. However, the OTF has taken the position that as a matter of policy it does not support strikes during the currency of contracts (as opposed to mass resignations upon their expiry):

> In the broader context of professional conduct OTF regards refusal of teachers to carry out the duties defined by the Regulations or the Schools Administration Act during the term of their contracts as strike action on the part of its members and deems such to be a breach of contract and contrary to the professional obligations of a teacher and therefore such strike action on the part of any group of members shall be considered unprofessional conduct and shall be treated in the same way as a breach of contract by an individual member.[16]

While this is an understandable position, the OTF has also taken the more conservative approach in its policy statements[17] that mass resignations ought not to take effect on December 31, presumably because of the disruptive effect of such action. It appears that the affiliates would be willing to contravene this policy if they felt driven to do so. Thus far they have not.

In one rather unusual case dealing with mass resignations, two public school associations issued graylistings warning that relations with the small Lakefield school board were unsatisfactory. The regular teachers then resigned, after giving appropriate notice. However, the board was able to employ replacements, many apparently from outside the province. The associations then sought the OTF's support to have the Department of Education withdraw the teaching certificates of the seventeen replacements hired by the Lakefield board. The OTF refused. This episode may indicate either the conservatism of the OTF or its considered judgment that public opinion is opposed to the compulsory nature of legislation requiring federation membership and that it would not countenance interference with the right of teachers to work where they wished. The long-term effects of this dispute with its graylistings and mass resignations apparently resulted in poor relations between parents, teachers, and the school board. More importantly, it may reveal the weakness of the entire scheme: if the OTF cannot, as a practical matter, invoke its ultimate sanction, it is a mere "paper tiger."

A possible from of reprisal against mass resignations is the blacklisting by school boards of all persons participating in the resignation movement. No "unfair labor practice" provisions exist to protect teachers against such a tactic. However, its effectiveness is greatly reduced in times of teacher shortages or in the event of mass resignations involving hundreds of teachers.

Another weapon which teachers could use quite effectively is "work-to-rule." However, this tactic is felt to be "unprofessional" as unduly interfering with classroom activity and as using innocent children as pawns; it would be employed with reluctance.

What are the prospects for future development in impasse resolution techniques for Ontario teachers? At the urging of its powerful Toronto local, an OSSTF committee was established to study teacher negotiation procedures and consider whether the present informal methods should be retained or whether the OSSTF should recommend legislation providing more formally structured collective bargaining and an arbitration procedure. No moves have been made to seek such legislation. Moreover, in February 1969 the OTF stated: "It is OTF policy that it is opposed to compulsory salary arbitration legislation. This does not rule out voluntary conciliation or a voluntary arbitration agreement between the parties."[18] The likelihood of a demand by teachers for the right to strike seems even more remote. At the OSSTF's annual convention in March 1969 the teachers rejected a proposal that its 31,000 members be asked in a referendum whether they wished to assert the right to strike and to obtain a more formal bargaining status.[19]

Nonetheless, there are signs of increased militancy among some groups of teachers, especially in urban areas. Whether these groups will continue to define themselves as self-restrained professionals or will wish to assert all of the power which their strategic position commands is really the crucial issue for future legislative developments.

THE SCOPE OF AGREEMENTS

When a settlement is reached between a board of education and a teacher association, no legislative provision compels the execution of a formal collective agreement. However, the parties normally incorporate their settlement in a document which governs their relationship until an agreed expiry date, usually August 31. The existing contracts between individual teachers represented in the negotiations and the board are then deemed to be varied so as to conform to the collective agreement reached with the association.

As there is no legislation providing for negotiation, so there is no legislation limiting the scope of negotiation or the contents of the agreement. The associations appear to take varying approaches to the question of scope. Presently the OSSTF "negotiates" on salary and fringe benefits but "conducts discussions" on other working conditions, e.g. workload, class size, and the hiring of lay assistants. The difference in terminology is, perhaps, of only transient significance, and future negotiations are almost bound to reach these other matters.[20] The other associations appear more willing to negotiate within a limited framework. Their demands concern only such conventional items as sick leave, gratuity plans, and medical coverage, in addition to salary.

The question of the scope of negotiations is becoming a question of great concern to affiliates. Teachers are generally considered to be professionals possessing specialized knowledge, and are increasingly university trained; they possess skills exercised in the interest and service of others and have power to discipline their own number. The OSSTF, in particular, contends that in accordance with its professional status, the teaching profession should be self-governing in a broader sense and should possess decision-making powers relating to such items as teacher qualification, curriculum, discipline, and evaluation. If this contention were accepted, the area of negotiations would embrace salary, fringe benefits, and such working conditions as class size, but would transfer decision-making with regard to educational policy and objectives to the teachers from the administrators. While the teachers have not thus far been particularly vocal in demands to diminish the policy-making role of either the local boards or the provincial Department of Education, their asserted prerogative to determine course content within the curriculum set by the department indicates the likely direction of their demands.

SECURITY OF TENURE

One area specifically provided for by legislation concerns the termination of both permanent and probationary contracts.[21] As noted, if either party to a permanent contract wishes to terminate it, whether prematurely or on one of the two dates provided in the contract, he must give written notice to the other party setting out his reasons for the termination. In the event that termination is not mutually agreed upon, either party may apply to the minister within fifteen days for the appointment of a tripartite board of reference. The minister may appoint or refuse to appoint the board within a further thirty days, but while his decision is pending and while the board is still sitting neither party may make a permanent commitment relating to employment. Before appointing the chairman of a board of reference (inevitably a county court judge) the minister may require the applicant to furnish security for costs, and will require both parties to name representatives to the board. The chairman must convene a hearing of the board of reference within thirty days of his appointment, and within seven days thereafter the board must report to the minister directing either continuance or discontinuance of the contract and making any other recommendation it deems advisable. Both the teacher and the school board are bound by the board's direction, noncompliance with which may be sanctioned, respectively, by loss of the teacher's certificate or loss of the board's provincial grant.

Legislation, however, does not assist the teacher covered by a probationary contract. A probationary contract provides for the employment of a teacher for a probationary period of not more than two years for a teacher with less than three years' experience before the commencement of the contract. The board, in terminating a probationary contract at the end of the year, need give no reasons for its actions, and the teacher has no recourse to a board of reference. The OTF has objected to this: "The following resolution was referred to the affiliates for a study and report to the Annual Meeting of the Board of Governors: 'That OTF seek an amendment to the probationary teachers' contract to require that the dismissal of a probationary teacher or the termination of the contract of a probationary teacher by a board shall state the reasons therefor.' "[22]

A further concern of the OTF relates to a school board's unilateral right to transfer teachers, a right which may be exercised in a positive fashion or as a means of forcing a teacher's resignation. The OTF has pressed for the right to have a board of reference available to determine, in the event of dispute, whether transfer is necessary and whether it works an undue hardship on the teacher. To date no such procedure has been established, but teachers are optimistic that their proposals will be accepted in the near future.

METROPOLITAN TORONTO: PROBLEMS OF TRANSITION

As indicated earlier, Metropolitan Toronto presents a special situation by reason of its unique "federal" system of government. As the province's most heterogeneous, and largest, city (about 30 percent of its total population), and as the home of the most radical teacher groups, Metropolitan Toronto provides an interesting study in teacher-trustee relations. Changes in the Toronto area are often greeted by vocal objection from the association central offices and more conservative factions within the teacher groups.

With the implementation of certain amendments to the Municipality of Metropolitan Act in 1966 which strengthened the financial control of the Metro board of education, it became clear that teachers would have to go to the place where budget decisions were effectively made in order to have their demands satisfied. Formerly, when negotiations took place in each of the constituent municipalities, the trustees and teachers justified their differing salary scales by maintaining that the government which raised money and paid the costs of education should have the right to set a local salary scale. After the implementation of a single Metro-wide tax scale and the formation of a single fund for educational finance, the inevitable logic of this argument became evident to both teachers and local boards of education. No longer could they bargain effectively on a one-by-one basis.

At first the movement to negotiations with the Metropolitan Toronto school board was bitterly opposed.[23] The OTF objected to teachers salaries being placed under Metro's jurisdiction: "It is OTF policy that it is opposed to any proposal to amend the Municipality of Metropolitan Toronto Act to put salaries of teachers under the jurisdiction of the Metropolitan School Board."[24] From the point of view of the teachers, Metro-wide salary negotiations would deprive them of the opportunity to "whipsaw" local boards and, by promoting uniformity in other matters, would reduce the ability of individual teachers to shop locally for more congenial work situations.

However, the OSSTF objected to the establishment of a single salary schedule for Metropolitan Toronto for an additional reason. Under the uniform scale a teacher would be remunerated both on the basis of his academic (technical) qualifications, which would permit horizontal movement from one category to the next, and professional teaching experience, which would permit vertical movement within any one category. An elementary school teacher might fall into any one of seven categories whereas a secondary school teacher would only be placed in one of the top four categories. Traditionally, the secondary school teachers initiate negotiations in Toronto in order to fix the top four levels. The elementary teachers normally accept these settlement figures, bargaining primarily on the bottom three levels. When, however, it was proposed that the teachers make their demands to the Metropolitan

Toronto school board the OSSTF refused initially to participate. In fact, 1127 center-city teachers executed resignations and delivered them to the association, as part of a mass resignation and pinklisting decision. However, the elementary teachers did agree to negotiate on a Metro-wide basis, and it soon appeared that they might make a settlement respecting all of the seven scales although the secondary teachers had no voice in negotiations. Thus the secondary teachers were pressured to enter negotiations with Metro in tandem with the elementary teachers, although the two teacher associations did bargain separately.

The six boards of education formed a single negotiating team. A staff of experts was then established to assist both parties and to provide a vehicle for informal mediation. However, although a settlement was reached with the elementary teachers, negotiations with the secondary school teachers broke down.

At this point, confronting a potential mass resignation and perhaps a strike, the parties agreed to appoint a mediator for the first time. After prolonged meetings the impasse was finally resolved. The experience has produced a generally favorable climate for future use of mediation, although both groups assert they hope to arrive at settlement without third-party assistance. However, these negotiations related only to salary. The parties continued to negotiate on fringe benefits (group life, health and accident, sick leave, retirement gratuity, and sabbatical leave), and these matters are not at the time of writing (six months later) resolved. A problem still to be confronted is whether negotiations on fringe benefits will take place at the same time as those relating to salary.

One area in which there has been cooperation between the Metropolitan Toronto school board, the six local boards, and the teachers is in the formation of the Quality Teaching Study. Committees were established with representatives from each group to study such issues as salary scheduling, merit pay, teacher workload, teacher training, and pupil-teacher ratio, and to set guidelines to improve the quality of education. The reports given by the committees are not binding on the boards or the federations and the matters discussed therein must ultimately be considered in the course of negotiations. It is important to note, in this connection, that the local boards do retain considerable autonomy, at least at present, to determine their own educational priorities insofar as they retain control over their budgets. Thus some boards may wish to develop special programs to serve a large immigrant population, while others may wish to emphasize special enrichment courses for the children of the suburban elite. These differences, which have survived the advent of centralized and uniform revenue raising, now offer boards the opportunity to compete for teachers as well as to serve their constituents better. It is to be hoped that these specialized responses to local conditions will also survive the move toward uniform measurement of quality and performance.

This brief description of the changing Metropolitan Toronto situation is significant because it highlights certain tensions in teacher collective bargaining: centralized financial control versus local autonomy in educational policy and militancy versus professional self-restraint.

CONCLUSION

The teachers of Ontario have engaged in a unique system of bargaining which has evolved as a result of their strength, their belief in a professional ethic, and their interest in improving the status of teachers. But while teacher association officials praise their system for its flexibility and maintain that necessary changes are few and relatively insignificant, some rank-and-file members and local officers have questioned its effectiveness. The associations' suggestions relating to the improvement of present practices are indeed quite mild. They include the development of negotiations on a more formal footing, to be concluded with an executed contract, definition of the authority of negotiating teams, inclusion of a wider range of working conditions within the ambit of negotiation, and greater use of voluntary mediation. While members have generally supported their leaders' contentions that teachers should maintain the present voluntary scheme of bargaining rather than construct a legislative framework, there are now strong internal pressures for change.

Teachers in the past have apparently subscribed to the belief that professionals do not belong to a "union" and they do not participate in "strike" actions.[25] However, in 1968 the Metropolitan Toronto Secondary School Teachers did agree to work through a committee to establish a common strategy for attaining union status with provision for compulsory arbitration. At the same time Toronto elementary school teachers were pressing for a single Toronto teacher union in which they would join with the secondary school teachers. While the provincial associations had traditionally opposed even suggestions of compulsory mediation and arbitration, the OSSTF's annual assembly in 1968 voted to eliminate official OSSTF opposition to such procedures.[26] However, despite this change of official policy, it is clear that the provincial executive was unhappy at any move toward unionization.[27] A check to the ambitions of the teacher activists was encountered in the spring of 1969. At that time OSSTF reasserted its traditional opposition to unionism and decided to seek neither legal bargaining status nor the right to strike. One of the advocates of the more conservative position noted that "the strength of our organization lies in our flexible policy."[28]

It seems evident, however, that the radicalization of teachers has not abated but merely shifted for tactical reasons to another issue. The OSSTF voted to study ways and means of withdrawing from the OTF on the ground that they had insufficient representation on the OTF governing body.

Further indications of disagreement between the parent federation, the OSSTF provincial association, and its locals was evident in the change in bargaining procedures in Metropolitan Toronto. While OTF has a strong policy indicating disagreement with negotiations on a Metro-wide basis, and while the OSSTF opposed it, it became increasingly evident that such a step was necessary. However, despite some willingness at the senior levels to discuss salaries with the Metro board, the local embracing center city secondary school teachers violently opposed the move. The internal fight was waged for some time until a mediator was appointed whose settlement proposals—on a Metro-wide basis—apparently found favor with the majority of all groups. Yet despite their differences the contending groups have so far maintained a solid front and do not appear to fear a breakaway movement or action in the form of wildcat strikes. Perhaps the common professional bond continues to serve them well.

The quiet atmosphere in Ontario (at least by comparison to some other Canadian and American jurisdictions) can be attributed to many factors. In the first place, as mentioned earlier, teachers consider that as professionals they should not participate in such assertive action as the strike. Second, public opinion toward a striking teacher is far from sympathetic and the fear is that little would be gained from such action. Third, the profession, having large numbers of women members whose immediate employment goals are short term, suffers from lethargy. These women have a great deal to lose from the consequences of a strike and little interest in its long-term effects. Fourth, some teachers fear that a more aggressive policy would invite government intervention and control. They wish to avoid all possibility of being labeled "civil servants." Fifth, teachers consider their responsibility to the pupil as being of primary importance. To involve the child in wage disputes is considered inexcusable by many. Finally, there are institutional loyalties which have prevented cooperation between the various teacher groups and reinforced male-female, primary-secondary, and public-parochial dichotomies and distinctions. Although these loyalties have inhibited the establishment of a simple strong teacher bargaining agency, there seems no willingness to replace the traditional associations.[29] Perhaps all of these considerations have contributed to the increasing tendency by individual teachers to participate in the general political arena. This may be seen as a vehicle for their talents, ideals, and desires for self-expression for which the present educational system and its collective bargaining procedures provide an inadequate outlet.

CHAPTER I

1. See generally, Carrothers, Collective Bargaining Law in Canada (1965), and Canadian Industrial Relations: Report of the Task Force on Labour Relations (H. D. Woods, Chairman, 1968).

2. Industrial Disputes Investigation Act, Stat. Can. 1907, c.20.

3. The first Canadian statute effectively establishing these rights was the Ontario Collective Bargaining Act, Stat. Ont. 1943, c.4. In 1944 the federal government preempted provincial legislative power over industrial relations in most industries by order-in-council P.C. 1003/44, passed under wartime emergency powers.

4. See Canadian Industrial Relations, *supra*, note 1 at 24ff.

5. A confidential and unpublished study of campus recruiting for the federal civil service would seem to corroborate this view, at least in relation to university graduates. Several persons connected with government personnel administration at both the federal and provincial levels also supported this impression in interviews.

6. Pineo and Porter, *Occupational Prestige in Canada,* (1967) 4 Can. Rev. of Soc. and Anthrop. 24.

7. Data in this section (and some of the inferences therefrom) are found in Hodgetts and Dwivedi, *The Growth of Government Employment in Canada,* (1969) 12 Can. Pub. Admin. 224.

8. See generally Porter, The Vertical Mosaic, c. XIV (1965).

9. *Toronto Daily Star,* Aug. 14, 1969.

10. *Toronto Daily Star,* Aug. 15, 1969.

11. The Trade Union Act, Stat. Sask. 1944, c. 207, s.2(f), now Rev. Stat. Sask. 1965, c.287, s.2(f).

12. Frankel, *Staff Relations in the Public Service: The Ghost of Sovereignty,* (1959) 2 Can. Pub. Admin. 65, at 67-68.

13. *Id.* at 69.

14. *Cf.* Finkelman, *When Bargaining Fails,* in Warner, ed., Collective Bargaining in the Public Service, 116 at 120 (1967): "To my mind, references to sovereignty in this connection have the effect . . . ot anaesthetizing intelligent examination of the relations between employers and employees. . . . Ideological concepts such as sovereignty are often no more than political myths functioning to preserve the existing social structure."

15. Rogers, The Law of Canadian Municipal Corporations, at 9-10 (1959).

16. Crown Agency Act, Rev. Stat. Ont. 1960, c.81; and see *R.* v. *O.L.R.B., ex parte Ontario Food Terminal Board,* (1962) 35 D.L.R. (2d) 6 (Ont. H.C.).

17. See *R.* v. *L.R.B. (B.C.) ex parte Simon Fraser University,* (1966) CLLC para. 14, 150 (B.C.S.C.); *National Union of Public Employees* v. *Board of Industrial Relations and Governors of University of Alberta,* (1963) 63 CLLC para. 15, 462 (Alta. S.C.).

CHAPTER II

1. Prior to 1966 the Ontario Labour Relations Act provided that a municipal council might by by-law bring itself outside of the statute, thus leaving its relations with employees to be governed by common law principles. This privilege was abolished by Stat. Ont. 1966, c. 76, s. 37. However, an analogous provision is still in force in Prince Edward Island, see the Industrial Relations Act, Stat. P.E.I. 1966, c. 19, s. l(j) (ii) (B), as amended. See also Frankel & Pratt, Municipal Labour Relations in Canada (1954).

2. See generally Arthurs, *Public Interest Labour Disputes in Canada,* (1967) 17 Buff. Law Rev. 39, and Essential Industry Disputes (Task Force Study No. 8, 1969).

3. See *Toronto Electricity Commissioners* v. *Snyder,* [1925] A.C. 396 (P.C.).

4. See generally Willes, A Study of Labour Relations Law Pertaining to the Bargaining Unit (unpublished LL.M. thesis, Osgoode Hall Law School, 1967); Herman, Determination of the Appropriate Bargaining Unit by Labour Relations Boards in Canada (1966).

5. See generally Simmons, Collective Bargaining at the Municipal Government Level in Canada (Draft Study prepared for the Task Force on Labour Relations, unpublished, March, 1968).

6. Labour Relations Act, Rev. Stat. Ont. 1960, c.202, s.54.

7. 1966 was a crisis year in Canadian municipal employment relations. Approximately 75,000 man days were lost as a result of 14 municipal employee strikes.

8. The Toronto Hydro Employees Union Dispute Act, 1965, Stat. Ont. 1965, c. 131; see also the Ontario Hydro Employees Union Dispute Act, Stat. Ont. 1961-62, c. 94, which similarly withdrew the right to strike (on an *ad hoc* basis) of employees of the provincially owned hydro-electric generating and distribution system.

9. *Op. cit. supra,* note 2.

CHAPTER III

1. This section includes adapted extracts from my article *Collective Bargaining in the Public Service of Canada: Bold Experiment or Act of Folly?* (1969) 67 Mich. L. Rev. 971.

2. Stat. Can. 1966-67, c.72.

3. See generally Report of the Preparatory Committee on Collective Bargaining in the Public Serivce, at 15ff. (Canada, 1965); Herman, *Collective Bargaining by Civil Servants* in Canada, [1966] Proc. Ann. Spring Meeting, I.R.R.A. 10 at 15ff., Vaison, *Collective Bargaining in the Federal Public Service: The Achievement of a Milestone in Personnel Relations,* (1969) 12 Can. Pub. Admin. 108.

4. Some indication of why postal employees were the first to organize may be found in the fact that, as of 1891, they had not received a wage increase for 32 years. See J. F. Maguire, *The Collective Agreement in the Federal Public Service* (unpublished address, Nov. 1968).

5. Discussed in greater detail, *infra.*

6. Civil Service Act, Stat. 1960-61, c.57, s.7. This 1961 legislation contemplated, in addition to consultation between the Civil Service Commission and the employee associations, direct consultation between the government and the associations.

7. Industrial Relations and Disputes Investigation Act, Rev. Stat. Can. 1952, c.157.

8. Report, *supra* note 3 at 36-37.

9. Here the distinction between "right" and "privilege" becomes razor thin.

10. See Herman, *supra* note 3 at 22, Love, *Proposals for Collective Bargaining in the Public Service: A Further Commentary, loc. cit. supra* note 3 at 24, 26.

11. See *infra* section on "Resolving Impasses: Arbitration or Strike?" It may be significant that the first lawful strike under the new statute was conducted by the very group of employees whose unlawful strike had prompted this fundamental change in the legislative scheme—the postal employees.

12. Section 2(o).

13. For example, the Dominion Coal Board and the National Energy Board are both part of the central administration, while the Atomic Energy Control Board is not; the National Film Board is a separate employer, while the National Gallery and the National Library are part of the central administration.

14. Industrial Relations and Disputes Investigation Act, *supra* note 7.

15. In fact the Treasury Board has existed since the establishment of the first Canadian parliament after Confederation in 1867; in a broad sense, it has always been responsible for government finances: see Love, *The Personnel Policy Branch of the Treasury Board: Its Mission, Character and Organization* (unpublished speech to Public Personnel Association, Ottawa, Oct., 1967). The statutory authority for the Treasury Board, and a definition of its function, is found in the Financial Administration Act, Rev. Stat. Can. 1952, c.116, as amended.

16. See Love, *op. cit. supra,* note 15; Davidson, *Critical Issues in Collective Bargaining in the Canadian Federal Service,* in Warner, ed., Collective Bargaining in the Public Service: Theory and Practice (1967).

17. Section 2(m), in addition to managerial personnel, exempts casual, part-time and temporary employees, persons compensated by fees of office, and uniformed members of the Royal Canadian Mounted Police.

18. Section 2(u) defines a "person employed in a managerial or confidential capacity" as someone who is in a position confidential to a federal judge, minister, or deputy minister, who are themselves excluded by section 2(m)(i), legal officers in the Department of Justice, and a person who is designated by the employer and found by the PSSRB "to be a person:

(iii) who has executive duties and responsibilities in relation to the development and administration of government programs,

(iv) whose duties include those of a personnel administrator or who has duties that cause him to be directly involved in the process of collective bargaining on behalf of the employer,

(v) who is required . . . to deal formally on behalf of the employer with a grievance . . .

(vi) who is not otherwise described . . . but who in the opinion of the Board should not be included in a bargaining unit by reason of his duties and responsibilities to the employer. . . ."

19. See Davidson, *op. cit. supra,* note 16, at 167-69.

20. The Professional Institute of the Public Service (PIPS), a long-established organization which represents several bargaining units, anticipated this problem by providing "affiliate membership" for persons ineligible for inclusion in a bargaining unit. See Proceedings, Special Joint Committee of the Senate and of the House of Commons on Employer-Employee Relations in the Public Service of Canada, at 416-17, 425-28. The Civil Service Association of Canada, a major service-wide organization, also sought to ensure the continued membership of non-bargaining unit personnel. *Id.* at 232-33.

21. Section 11(1).

22. Section 11(2)-(3).

23. *See* text *infra.*

24. *See* text *infra.*

25. The Pay Research Bureau is also administered under the PSSRB.

26. Section 60(1).

27. Section 60(2).

28. Section 92.

29. Section 17(4).

30. Report, *supra* note 3, at 25.

31. The caliber of appointments made to the PSSRB and its adjunct bodies likewise helps to explain their impartiality and independence. The chairman of the PSSRB—the central figure in the entire scheme—is Jacob Finkelman, a former law teacher and for many years chairman of the Ontario Labour Relations Board, the nation's busiest labor tribunal. The chairman of the Arbitration Tribunal is Justice Andre Montpetit of the Superior Court of Quebec, an experienced labor mediator.

32. Stat. Can. 1966-67, c.71, s.2.

33. Report, *supra,* note 3 at 26.

34. Section 6.

35. Section 8(1).

36. Section 8(2).

37. Section 20.

38. Section 21.

39. Section 106. The statute does not explicitly indicate that unfair practices or violations of remedial orders are offenses, although reference is made in section 106 to "prosecution arising out of an alleged failure to observe any prohibition contained in section 8. . . ." Section 107 of the Criminal Code, Stat. Can. 1953-54, c.51, provides: "Everyone who . . . contravenes an Act of the Parliament of Canada . . . is, unless some penalty or punishment is expressly provided by law, guilty of an indictable offense and is liable to imprisonment for two years." Presumably, prosecution under this section is contemplated; certainly the legislative intention was that prosecution should be the ultimate enforcement procedure. See Proceedings, *op. cit. supra,* note 20 at 917.

40. Section 49.

41. Section 39(3) explicitly makes ineligible for certification any union "which discriminates against any employee because of sex, race, national origin, colour, or religion."

42. Section 40(1)(a).

43. Section 26 authorizes the Public Service Commission to "specify and define the several occupational groups within each occupational category" established by the statute. During the initial certification period these occupational groups were intended to be coterminous with bargaining units.

44. Section 26(5).

45. Section 32.

46. Section 32(2).

47. Section 50.

48. Section 36.

49. Section 2(w).

50. Section 72(1).

51. This point is made explicit by section 101(1)(b).

52. *Regina* v. *C.P.R., ex rel. Zambri,* [1962] S.C.R. 609.

53. The issue was raised, and avoided, in *A.G. British Columbia* v. *Ellsay and B.C. Government Employees' Association,* (1959) CLLC 15, 262 (BCSC).

54. Section 79.

55. In the same case the parties were able to agree that civilian employees involved in maintaining communications for the armed services, police, the Department of External Affairs, and government coast guard, search, rescue and weather ships would be designated. In certain cases, the employer undertook that their functions would be restricted, in the event of a strike, to activities needed to preserve these essential public functions.

56. Section 25.

57. Section 38 provides for the changing of the union's election. However, it is unclear whether this section would permit a bargaining agent to reelect (prior to the commencement of negotiations) once it has officially recorded its choice with the PSSRB.

58. See Gauthier, *Pay Research and Employee Relations in the Canadian Federal Service* in Warner and Donovan, eds., Practical Guidelines to Public Pay Administration, at 156 (1965); Wilkins, *The Pay Research Bureau,* (Sept., 1967) Civ. Serv. Rev. 1; PSSRB, First Annual Report, at 44ff. (1967-68).

59. Wilkins, Address to Western Canadian Cities Personnel and Labour Relations Workshop (unpublished, Feb., 1969).

60. Under section 52, either party may apply to the chairman of the PSSRB for "the assistance of a conciliator in reaching agreement," although appointment of a conciliator is not mandatory.

61. See generally sections 77 to 89.

62. Section 68 provides:

"In the conduct of proceedings before it and in rendering an arbitral award in respect of a matter in dispute the Arbitration Tribunal shall consider

    (a) the needs of the Public Service for qualified employees;

    (b) the conditions of employment in similar occupations outside the Public Service, including such geographic, industrial or other variations as the Arbitration Tribunal may consider relevant;

158

(c) the need to maintain appropriate relationships in the conditions of employment as between different grade levels within an occupation and as between occupations in the Public Service;

(d) the need to establish terms and conditions of employment that are fair and reasonable in relation to the qualifications required, the work performed, the responsibility assumed and the nature of the services rendered; and

(e) any other factor that to it appears to be relevant to the matter in dispute."

63. Section 71.

64. Most of what follows is a composite impression formed by the author as a result of formal interviews and informal discussions with various participants, and of newspapers and periodical reports. It is obviously subject to all the risks associated with this technique of information gathering and interpretation.

65. See the statement of Claude Edwards, PSAC president, *Effect of Collective Bargaining on Staff Associations*, (Mar. 1968) 41 Civ. Serv. Rev. 32: "I think the central body [the Alliance] will be given clear jurisdiction over central issues and overall disciplining jurisdiction over the Components. The role of the bargaining groups will become stronger and we may see them becoming politically structured. If this does happen, they will reduce the power of the Components on policy decisions relative to the collective bargaining issue. This to me seems inevitable if the bargaining continues on an occupational group basis. . . . If we don't hang together we will all hang apart."

66. (July 1968) 47 Professional Public Service.

67. Report, *supra* note 3 at 34.

68. *Ibid.*

69. Sections 56, 70(2), 86(2).

70. Section 49.

71. Section 2(h).

72. Section 70(1).

73. Sections 70(3), 86(3).

74. Stat. Can. 1966-67, c.71, section 8.

75. Sections 10, 22, 31.

76. Sections 13 *et seq.* (promotion); section 31 (demotion); section 29 (layoff).

77. Public Service Act, section 12(3).

78. Section 112.

79. Sections 58, 72.

80. Report, *supra* note 3 at 37.

81. Sections 56, 74.

82. Section 26(6).

83. *Ibid.*

84. Section 57.

85. Sections 26, 41.

86. Section 90.

87. Section 91.

88. Section 2(p)(i) provides that managerial personnel are eligible to submit and process grievances. Ironically, the first grievance to be

adjudicated after the legislation came into force was that of a personnel manager who was found to have been improperly discharged, *Caron* case, file 166C-1 (unreported, Sept. 21, 1967).

89. Sections 90(2), 91(2).

90. Section 98.

91. Section 92, 94.

92. Section 93, 94(2)(b).

93. Section 94(2)(a).

94. To some extent this is achieved by the exercise of the chief adjudicator's power to determine whether a grievance falls within the jurisdictional limits defined in the act, and whether it is timely, PSSRB Regulations and Rules of Procedure, SOR/67-200, as amended by SOR/68-114, section 53. As well, all "policy" grievances (i.e. those filed by the employer or the bargaining agent) must be heard by the chief adjudicator, PSSRA, section 98.

95. Section 97. Subsections (2) and (3) provide that the board may recover some or all of the costs of normal adjudication, but to date this has not been done.

96. *Caron* case, *supra* note 88.

97. Section 96(4)(5).

98. Section 96(6).

99. Section 23 provides for review by the PSSRB only of a "question of law or jurisdiction" arising in connection with grievance adjudication. Such questions may not be raised in the course of a proceeding to enforce the decision of an adjudicator, section 96(6).

100. Section 100.

101. Section 90.

102. With the decrease in the transportation of mail by rail, the railway mail clerks have been in the process of being integrated into other areas of employment in the post office. This process created difficulties in such matters as seniority and accelerated the split between the railway mail clerks and the other groups.

103. Montreal, Ottawa, Toronto, Winnipeg, and Vancouver.

104. Canada Post Office, (1968) Annual Report 8.

105. House of Commons Debates (*HCD*), September 30, 1968, 560.

106. *Supra,* note 7.

107. Report of the Royal Commission of Inquiry into Working Conditions in the Post Office Department (Mr. Justice Andre Montpetit, Commissioner, 1966), hereinafter "the Montpetit Report."

108. The Royal Commission on Government Organization (J. G. Glassco, Chairman, 1962).

109. *Ibid.,* Vol. 3, p. 329.

110. See e.g. *HCD*, April 30, 1964, 2771 (Mr. Scott).

111. See *HCD,* June 14, 1965, 2339 (Mr. Starr); April 2, 1965 (Mr. Valade).

112. *Globe and Mail* (editorial), July 27, 1965.

113. Figures taken from *Interim Report of Commission of Inquiry into the Increases in Rates of Pay for Civil Servants in Group D,* (J. C. Anderson, Commissioner, 1965). Salary schedule appended. In 1965, "Group D" employees also included custom and immigration officials, certain technicians, draftsmen, certain semiskilled workers and tradesmen, foremen, and supervisors.

114. Report, *supra* note 113.
115. See the *Civil Service Act,* Stat. Can. 1960-61, c.57, ss.50-53. By s.50, an employee of the civil service held his position "during the pleasure of Her Majesty," and an employee absent from duty without leave for one week could be declared by the deputy minister "to have abandoned his position" (s.53). Finally, by s.50(2), it was declared that nothing in the act affected the right or power of the Governor in Council "to remove or dismiss any employee."
116. *Globe and Mail,* July 27, 1965.
117. *Ibid.*
118. *Globe and Mail,* Aug. 9, 1965.
119. *Globe and Mail* (editorial), Aug. 9, 1965.
120. Report, *supra* note 107.
121. In order to guard against theft from the mails, employees working were supervised through peepholes which looked down on the work area.
122. Montpetit Report, *supra* note 107 at 17-27.
123. *Ibid.,* 17.
124. *Ibid.,* 29-35.
125. *Globe and Mail* (editorial), Oct. 24, 1966.
126. Statement by Postmaster General Kierans, *HCD,* Nov. 13, 1968, 2676-77.
127. Proceedings of the Special Joint Committee of the Senate and of the House of Commons on Employer-Employee Relations in the Public Service of Canada. (Senator Maurice Bourget, and Mr. Jean T. Richard M.P., Joint Chairmen, 1966), *supra* note 20.
128. See Proceedings, *supra* note 20, Brief of CUPW at 300-10; of LCUC at 313-26; questioning of Decarie at 571-95; of Kay at 603-17.
129. *Ibid.,* 574.
130. *Ottawa Citizen* (editorial), Nov. 8, 1966.
131. *The Strike of the Postal Workers,* (Dec. 1968) Postal Tribune. (The Postal Tribune was until the end of 1968 the monthly organ of CUPW. It is now defunct.)
132. *President's Report* (May 1968). Postal Tribune.
133. May 30, 1968.
134. *Toronto Daily Star,* (editorial) Aug. 1, 1968; *Toronto Telegram,* (editorial) Aug. 1, 1968.
135. *Globe and Mail,* Aug. 1, 1968.
136. Aug. 1, 1968 (editorial).
137. (Dec. 1, 1968) Postal Tribune 37.
138. *Re the Council of Postal Unions and the Treasury Board,* file 169-2-1 (unreported, April 30, 1969; Martin, Chief Adjudicator).
139. *Ibid.,* 32, 37.
140. *Levesque* case, file 166-2-104; *Southern* case, file 166-2-103 (unreported, May 16, 1969, Martin, Chief Adjudicator).

CHAPTER IV

1. Firemen perform a similar vital public safety function and operate under a compulsory arbitration statute similar to that described *infra* relating to policemen. See Fire Departments Act, Rev. Stat. Ont. 1960, c. 149, s.6.

2. Rev. Stat. Ont. 1960, c. 298 (as amended).

3. Stat. Ont. 1961-62, c. 121.

4. *Reference re Power of Municipal Council to Dismiss a Chief Constable or Other Police Officer Without a Hearing,* (1957) 7 D.L.R. (2d) 222 (Ont. C.A.).

5. *Id.* at 225.

6. Police Act, s.7; but see the Municipality of Metropolitan Toronto Act, Rev. Stat. Ont. 1960, c. 260, s.196 (1), as amended by Stat. Ont. 1968, c. 80, s.12, which provides a five-man commission for the province's largest municipality, comprising the chairman of the metropolitan council, another member of the council, two judicial officers, and a "public" member.

7. Significantly, the president of the Metropolitan Toronto Police Association, P. C. Sydney Brown, favors the ombudsman concept through which, presumably, citizen complaints against the Police Commission might be vetted. Brown is also president of the International Conference of Police Associations and his position is in direct contrast to the anticitizen review stand of most of the U. S. police organizations which comprise the bulk of the ICPA membership.

8. Police Act, ss. 13, 16, as amended by Stat. Ont. 1965, c. 99 and Stat. Ont. 1966, c. 118.

9. Police Act, ss. 32, 35, as amended *supra,* note 8.

10. Ont. Reg. 110/69.

11. An Act to Amend the Police Act, Bill 178 (Ontario, 2d. Sess., 28th Legislature, 1968-69).

12. *R. v. Ont. L.R.B., ex parte Canadian Union of Public Employees, Local 543,* (1964) 45 D.L.R. (2d) 202 at 205 (Ont. H. C.).

13. Stat. Ont. 1965, c. 99, s.6(1).

14. *Beckett* v. *City of Sault Ste. Marie Police Commissioners,* [1968] 1 O.R. 633 at 641.

15. See generally Police Act, ss. 27-35.

16. Section 60.

17. Section 27.

18. In the case of police forces comprising less than twenty members, a single arbitrator is provided in lieu of a tripartite board.

19. See Debates of the Legislature of Ontario, June 10, 19, 20, 26, 1969.

20. Mr. Sydney Brown, president of the MTPA, the PAO, the Canadian Police Association and (noted *supra*) the ICPA, holds the rank of constable on the Toronto force, from which he is on leave.

21. Debates, *supra* note 19, June 20, 1969, at 5942.

22. Submission of PAO with respect to Bill 178, 1.

23. See the speeches of members Sopha (6340, 6349), Reid (6351), and Renwick (6345), *op cit. supra,* note 19.

24. *Op. cit. supra,* note 22, 2.

25. *Re MTPA and the Metropolitan Board of Commissioners of Police,* (unreported, 1968, Ont. H.C.).

26. Rev. Stat. Que. 1964, c. 141, s. 93.

27. Section 32, as amended by Stat. Ont. 1968-69, c. 97.

28. Section 33.

29. Ont. Reg. 110/69.

30. PAO Submission to the Hon. Arthur A. Wishart, Minister of Justice and Attorney-General of Ontario (unpublished, April 15, 1969).
31. Letter to the Editor, *Toronto Globe and Mail*, 6, Aug. 7, 1969.
32. *Ibid.*

CHAPTER V

1. Report on Collective Bargaining in the Ontario Government Service (Judge Walter Little, Special Adviser, 1969), hereinafter "The Little Report."
2. Stat. Ont. 1878, c.2.
3. Stat. Ont. 1918, c.5.
4. Stat. Ont. 1947, c.89.
5. Stat. Ont. 1961-62, c.121, as amended by Stat. Ont. 1962-63, c.118; Stat. Ont. 1965, c.100; Stat. Ont. 1966, c.130; Stat. Ont. 1968, c.110.
6. Public Service Act, Stat. Ont. 1961-62, c.121, s. 1(da) as amended.
7. For purposes other than collective bargaining, the Public Service Act distinguishes between the "classified service" (appointed by the Civil Service Commission) and the "unclassified service" (appointed by a Minister), sections 1(b) (h), 4a. However, all "crown employees" (the generic term) may be covered by negotiations under the act, section 19a (4) (b).
8. *Collective Bargaining in the Ontario Government Service, a Brief Review* (Staff Relations Branch, Treasury Board, unpublished memorandum Dec. 5, 1968).
9. Sections 2-4.
10. The following information is taken, unless indicated to the contrary, from a CSAO publication: *The Civil Service Association of Ontario (Inc.): A Review of its Formation and Growth,* and from interviews with CSAO staff.
11. Section 19a, discussed *infra* under "Determining Issues of Representation."
12. Ontario Public Service Superannuation Act, Stat. Ont. 1920, c.5, now Rev. Stat. Ont. 1960, c.332.
13. As of 1969 approximately 27,640 civil servants were subject to voluntary checkoff, Little Report, *supra* note 1, at 9.
14. As of 1969 CSAO had a total membership of 33,240, among some 50,000 eligible employees, Little Report, *supra* note 1, at 7-8.
15. See the Report and Recommendations of the Associations Study Group on Organization of the Civil Service of Ontario (Inc.) (unpublished, 1968).
16. See Crispo and Arthurs, *Labour Unrest in Canada: Some Implications of Recent Experience,* (1968) 23 Ind. Rel. 237.
17. See Public Services Act, sections 19a (1)(b) and 19b(2)(c), respectively providing for the appointment of staff side members on the Joint [negotiating] Council and the Civil Service Arbitration Board. The sole statutory exception relates to special negotiation and arbitration machinery for the Ontario Provincial Police, see Public Services Act, section 20(1)(r) and Ont. Reg. 213/65.

18. The refusal of the province to continue to recognize their union, CUPE, and their forceable integration into the CSAO bargaining unit, resulted in a strike. As part of the settlement of this strike, the matter was referred to Judge Little, who rejected the CUPE position. The CUPE position was supported *inter alia* by the *Toronto Globe & Mail,* a normally conservative paper. (See editorial, Jan. 18, 1968.)

19. Report of the Royal Commission on Employer-Employee Relations in the Public Services of New Brunswick (S. J. Frankel, Commissioner, 1967).

20. Little Report, *supra* note 1, at 30.

21. *Id.* at 31.

22. Ont. Reg. 403/69.

23. As confirmatory evidence of this prediction, CASO's chief rival, CUPE, announced that it was reducing "initiation" fees for provincial government employees from $5.00 to $2.00, and excusing them from the payment of monthly dues until a collective agreement could be negotiated. By this move CUPE hoped to demonstrate numerical strength which would deter the government from implementing the Little Report's recommendations. It failed to do so, and a CUPE official remarked that government employees "will be saddled with a company union for a long time to come."

24. Little Report, *supra* note 1 at 8.

25. *Id* at 28-29.

26. "The situation in Ontario is relatively stabilized due to the existence of established appropriate units," Little Report, *supra* note 1 at 30.

27. Little Report, *supra* note 1 at 8.

28. CSAO Study Group, *supra* note 14 at 22.

28. CSAO Study Group, *supra* note 14 at 22.

29. Little Report, *supra* note 1, at 11.

30. *Id.* at 12.

31. *Id.* at 14-15.

32. Public Service Act, sections 4(a)(d) and 20(1)(b).

33. Section 19a(4)(b), (7).

34. Ont. Reg. 190/62, s.17 and s.24(1), Ont. Reg. 252/63, s.1. See also (Mar. 1969) 4 CSAO News 2.

35. Little Report, *supra* note 1 at 32.

36. *Why Arbitration? The Story,* (Aug 1968) 3 CSAO News 1.

37. Public Service Act, s.19a, deals with the composition and duties of the Joint Council.

38. Section 19a(7).

39. See *Collective Bargaining in the Ontario Government Service, A Brief Review, op. cit. supra,* note 8.

Year	Number of Meetings
1963 (7 mos.)	·9
1964	11
1965	15
1966	11
1967	5
1968	5

40. CSAO Submission to Judge Little, 21.

41. Little Report, *supra* note 1 at 34.
42. Public Service Act, s.19a(8).
43. Section 19b(1).
44. *Mediation: Catalyst to Collective Bargaining,* (Apr. 1967) 2 CSAO News 3.
45. (Summer 1967) The Trillium 4.
46. Public Service Act, s.19b(1a).
47. Section 19b(3).
48. Report of the Royal Commission Inquiry into Labour Disputes, at 111 (Hon. I. C. Rand, Commissioner, Ontario, 1968).
49. Little Report, *supra* note 1 at 42.
50. *Special Issue on the Little Report,* (June, 1969) 4 CSAO News 1; see also CSAO submission, *op. cit. supra,* note 40 at 23.
51. Little Report, *supra* note 1, at 42-43.
52. See ch. III, *supra.*
53. Section 19a(8).
54. CSAO submission, *op cit. supra,* note 40 at 13-14.
55. Little Report, *supra* note 1 at 44.
56. Ont. Reg. 190/62, ss.29-42.
57. *Grievance Solves Salary Hassle,* (May 1969) 4 CSAO News 3.
58. (Summer 1969) The Trillium.
59. Little Report, *supra* note 1 at 35.
60. F. F. Schindeler, Responsible Government in Ontario, 265 (1969).

CHAPTER VI

1. Department of Education Act, Rev. Stat. Ont. 1960, c.94.
2. Reflecting a preconfederation constitutional compromise, Ontario has a dual system of publicly supported primary schools. The "public school" system is open to all school age children, while the "separate school" system is open to the children of local Catholic or Protestant minorities whose parents opt out of the public school system. At the secondary school level there is a single "public" school system. However, for purposes of this study no relevant distinctions exist between the two streams, both of which are governed by similar, if not identical, legislation and informal arrangements. See Separate Schools Act, Rev. Stat. Ont. 1960, c. 368; Secondary Schools and Boards of Education Act, Rev. Stat. Ont. 1960, c. 362; Public Schools Act, Rev. Stat. Ont. 1960, c. 330; Schools Administration Act, Rev. Stat. Ont. 1960, c. 361. c. 361.
3. Municipality of Metropolitan Toronto Act, Rev. Stat. Ont. 1960 c. 260, as amended by Stat. Ont. 1966, c. 96; see also Report of the Royal Commission on Metropolitan Toronto (H. Carl Goldenberg, Commissioner, Ontario, 1965).
4. Rev. Stat. Ont. 1960, c.202.
5. Information in this section is derived from interviews and from We, The Teachers of Ontario (OTF Information Handbook, Jan. 1969).
6. Teaching Profession Act, Stat. Ont. 1960, c. 393.
7. OTF Bylaw xiii.

8. Details of the organization and membership of the affiliates is found in We, The Teachers of Ontario, *op. cit. supra*, note 5 at 84-108.

9. OTF Policy Resolution 14 reproduced in We, The Teachers of Ontario, *op. cit. supra*, note 5 at 61.

10. Ont. Reg. 63/55, ss. 19-21, made under The Teaching Profession Act, reproduced in We, The Teachers of Ontario, *supra* note 5 at 28-33.

11. Lieberman and Moskow, Collective Negotiations for Teachers, 163-84 (1966).

12. Schools Administration Act, s.22(2)(g).

13. Ont. Reg. 63/55, s. 18(1)(c).

14. OTF Bylaw I.

15. See the Department of Education Act and regulations thereunder establishing a standard "Permanent Teacher's Contract," Rev. Reg. Ont. 1960, Reg. 105, cl. 6; see also We, The Teachers of Ontario, *op. cit. supra*, note 5 at 70-80.

16. OTF Salary Policy, (Feb. 1969) 13 OTF Reporter 15; see also We, The Teachers of Ontario, *op. cit. supra*, note 5 at 64.

17. OTF Policy Resolution 14 (11)(12), reproduced in We, The Teachers of Ontario, *op. cit. supra*, note 5 at 64.

18. (Feb. 1969) 13 OTF Reporter 12.

19. *Toronto Globe & Mail*, March 20, 1969.

20. After this text was written, negotiations involving the Toronto secondary school teachers in the spring of 1970 raised directly, and as a condition precedant to further discussions, the issue of teacher/pupil ratios.

21. Schools Administration Act, ss. 24-33.

22. Hidgins, *From the Secretary's Desk*, (May, 1968) 11 OTF Reporter 3.

23. *Toronto Telegram*, March 7, 1967.

24. (Feb. 1969) 13 OTF Reporter 15.

25. For example, C. McClaffrey, OSSTF president, opposed hiring of teachers from Quebec or Great Britain on the grounds that teaching in those jurisdictions is not a "profession," and that teachers there have trade union backgrounds, *Toronto Daily Star*, March 30, 1967.

26. *Toronto Daily Star*, Nov. 18, 1968.

27. *Toronto Daily Star*, Nov. 19, 1968.

28. *Toronto Globe and Mail*, Mar. 20, 1969.

29. Such a move was recommended in Living and Learning: Report of the Provincial Committee on Aims and Objectives of Education (Ontario, 1968).